Advocacy
The Companion
Handbook

A Guide to Advocacy and Lobbying in Canada and the United States

By Steven Christianson

Advocacy – The Companion Handbook:
A Guide to Advocacy and Lobbying in Canada and the United States

by Steven Christianson

Published by
Henley Point
Toronto, Canada
www.henleypoint.ca

The information contained in this publication is provided for informational and referential purposes only, and should not be construed as legal advice on any subject matter.

Neither the publisher nor the author is responsible for websites (or their content) that are not owned by the publisher or author.

Cover design by Josée Scalabrini and Henley Point Productions

ISBN: 978-1-7778-3470-8

CONTENTS

ABOUT *THE COMPANION*

Advocacy – The Companion Handbook is a companion book to *Advocacy: Explained!* This companion is a reference manual, a planning journal, and a directory. It features a distillation of the main concepts and ideas from the larger book, *Advocacy: Explained!*, while condensing key information that would be critical for any practitioner.

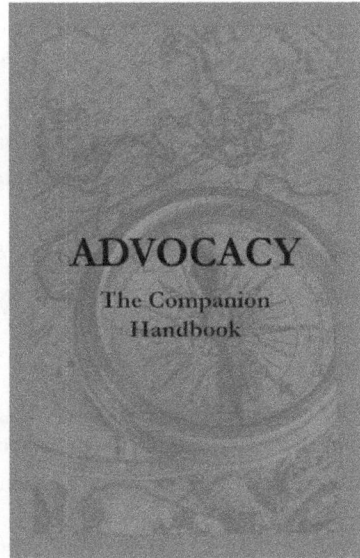

Advocacy: Explained! For those who want the theory, the historical and international comparisons of legislation, and a larger, more conceptual picture of advocacy, lobbying and government relations.

Advocacy – The Companion: For those who want a guide on planning, preparing and organizing, on navigating the circuitry and getting to the target of power, as well as a compact directory of key advocacy and lobby offices in the US and Canada.

1

ADVOCACY AND LOBBYING

What is Advocacy?
Advocacy aims to …
Introduce
Change
Oppose
Eliminate.

Is it Advocacy or Lobbying?

Advocacy is the larger concept, of which lobbying is a subset. Corporate lobbying is a subset within lobbying itself. To draw an analogy: advocacy is the "retail department store", and lobbying represents a department within that store – a department that includes specialty products like corporate lobbying.

There are many terms associated with professionals and campaigners who try to influence policy and make change: advocates, lobbyists, government relations specialists, public affairs advisors, influencers, and many more. Bottom line: if you are working to help influence policy and make change, you probably have to register with a government office through some definition of "lobbying". Be safe, rather than incurring a fine or penalty.

GLOSSARY

Advocacy Groups
Advocacy groups, also known as interest groups, special interest groups or pressure groups, use various forms of advocacy in order to influence public opinion and ultimately policy. They play an important role in the development of political and social systems.

Alliance
An alliance is a union or association formed for mutual benefit, between organizations. The relationship of an alliance is based on an affinity in interests, nature, or qualities.

Amendment
A change proposed to a motion, bill or committee report with the intention of improving it or providing an alternative.

Appropriation
This refers to the legislation to provide the money required for governmental programs, agencies, boards, and commissions.

Bill
A proposal for a law that is to be considered by a legislature.

Brief
This is a document summarizing important information on a specific subject including the background and purpose of an advocacy campaign.

Briefing Note
A briefing note, or briefing paper, is a document that is used to inform decision makers (a board, a politician, etc.) on current issues. It is a clear and concise document that summarizes an issue and identifies key pieces of information, such as a situation that needs to be addressed as well as its financial implications.

Budget Advocacy

Government budgets offer a path for committed financial resources and government expenditures (tax-related or otherwise). This type of advocacy is a trajectory that focuses on the budget processes of government.

Bureaucratic Advocacy

Bureaucratic advocacy works through systems of consultation as regards specific regulations.

Cabinet

This is the executive decision-making body of the government, typically comprised of the Prime Minister (or Premier) and the Ministers responsible.

Caucus

A group composed of all Senators and Members/Representatives (both elected and appointed) from the same political party.

Coalition

In civil society, "coalition" connotes a group effort or a population of people coming together who believe strongly in their cause. The term also describes alliances between civil society organizations, such as labour unions, community organizations, and religious institutions.

Committees (Canadian context)

There are three main types of committees: legislative committees, which examine bills after second reading in the House; standing committees, which study certain issues, documents, departments or estimates throughout the duration of the Parliament; and special committees, which are appointed to inquire into specific matters.

Conflict of Interest and Ethics Commissioner (of Canada)

The Conflict of Interest and Ethics Commissioner of Canada is an entity of the Parliament of Canada. The commissioner is an independent officer of Parliament, who administers the Conflict of Interest Act and the Conflict of Interest Code for Members of the House of Commons and is supported in this role by the Office of the Conflict of Interest and Ethics Commissioner. The Conflict of Interest Act for public office holders (ministers, ministers of state, Parliamentary secretaries, ministerial staff and governor-in-council appointees) and the Conflict of Interest Code for Members of the House of Commons set out a number of obligations and prohibit various activities that involve conflicts between private and public interests, or have the potential to do so.

Congressional District

Congressional districts are the 435 regions from which voting representatives are elected to the U.S. House of Representatives. After the decennial census population counts and apportionment of congressional seats, states are required to define and delineate their own congressional districts for the purpose of electing members to the House of Representatives. Each congressional district is expected to be equal in population to all other congressional districts in a state.

Demonstration (political)

A political demonstration is an action by a mass group or collection of groups of people in favour of a political or other cause, or people participating in a protest against a cause of concern; it often consists of walking in a mass march formation and either beginning with or meeting at a designated endpoint, or rally, to hear speakers. Demonstrations are different from mass meetings.

Deputation

A deputation is a written or verbal presentation that residents, community groups or any interested party can present to a committee or board of a government. Deputations can represent effective ways in which to educate committee members and staff on a given issue. Deputations also secure one's point of view on the public record. Deputations are also referred to as presentations or expert testimony, depending on the nature of the committee or board, and sometimes on the level of government.

Elected Officials

In Canada

- MP is a federal Member of Parliament.
- MPP is a Member of Provincial Parliament (Ontario legislature only)
- MNA is a Member of the National Assembly (Quebec legislature only)
- MHA is a Member of the House of Assembly (Newfoundland & Labrador legislature only)
- MLA is a Member of the Legislative Assembly (all other provinces and territories).

In the United States

- Member of Congress, Congressman, Congresswoman, Representative, Senator
- Congress is a descriptive term that refers to the collective body of legislators, from the both the Senate and the House of Representatives.
- Congressman/Congresswoman is a member of the House of Representatives. Representative is also used.
- Senators are elected members of Congress, serving in the Senate, but are not usually referred to as Congressmen or Congresswomen.

Electoral Advocacy

This form of advocacy focuses on speaking out on particular issues during campaigns for elected office. Tactics can include many activities, such as providing information to candidates, seeking support from candidates, and promotional and media campaigns.

Filibuster
This is a time-delaying tactic used in an effort to delay, modify or defeat a bill or amendment.

Focus Groups
This is a method of qualitative research in which a small group of individuals are asked about their beliefs and opinions regarding an advocacy agenda item.

Governor General
This is the Queen's representative in Canada. No legislative bill can be enacted as a law without the Royal Assent (signed approval) by the Governor General.

Ideological Advocacy
Ideological advocacy is one of the more diffuse forms of advocacy, in that this usually involves groups employing public protests, mass meetings and demonstrations to advance their ideas.

Interest Groups
Interest groups, also known as special interest groups or pressure groups, use various forms of advocacy in order to influence public opinion and ultimately policy. They play an important role in the development of political and social systems.

Issue Advocacy
Issue advocacy involves considerable effort in public education, and frequently relies on methods associated with public or media affairs.

Joint Committee
A committee made up of a proportionate number of members of both the House of Commons/House of Representatives and the Senate. It may be either a standing joint committee or a special joint committee.

Legislative Advocacy

Legislative advocacy relies more than anything on the processes through the provincial, state, territorial or federal governments, which typically include committee hearings, presentations and deputations, as part of a strategy to create change.

Lieutenant Governor

In Canada, a lieutenant governor is the vice-regal representative in a provincial jurisdiction of the Canadian monarch and head of state, Queen Elizabeth II. The lieutenant-governor alone is also constitutionally mandated to summon the legislature. Beyond that, the viceroy carries out the other conventional parliamentary duties in the sovereign's stead, including reading the Speech from the Throne and proroguing and dissolving parliament. The lieutenant-governor also grants Royal Assent in the Queen's name; legally, he or she has three options: grant Royal Assent (making the bill law), withhold Royal Assent (vetoing the bill), or reserve the bill for the signification of the governor general's pleasure. If the governor general withholds the Queen's assent, the sovereign may within two years disallow the bill, thereby annulling the law in question.

Lobby Register

A Lobby Registry, also named Lobbyist Registry, Register for Lobby Transparency or Registry of Lobbyists, is a public database, in which information about lobbying actors and key data about their actions can be accessed.

Lobbying

In politics, lobbying, persuasion, or interest representation is the act of lawfully attempting to influence the actions, policies, or decisions of government officials, most often legislators or members of regulatory agencies. Distinctions include corporate lobbying, direct lobbying and grassroots lobbying.

Mass Advocacy
Mass advocacy takes shape through action taken by large groups (via petitions or demonstrations, for example).

Mass Meeting
A mass meeting is a type of deliberative assembly, which in a publicized or selectively distributed notice known as the call of the meeting - has been announced. A mass meeting is called to take appropriate action on a particular problem or toward a particular purpose stated by the meeting's sponsors; and is open to everyone interested in the stated problem or purpose.

Media Advocacy
Media advocacy is usually the strategic use of mass media to advance a social or public policy initiative.

Members' Statements
In Canada, Members' Statements, or Statements by Members, is a daily allotment of time in a legislative assembly when Members of Parliament who are not Cabinet Ministers can speak for up to one minute or two minutes each on matters they consider to be important (including causes and organizations specific to their constituencies).

Omnibus Bill
This is a packaged piece of legislation that results when a group of bills (usually on related topics) are combined into a single bill for consideration by a legislature.

Partnership (political)
A partnership is an arrangement between two or more people, or organizations, to oversee administrative and operational matters.

Para-Public Sector
Those institutions that are funded (in whole or in part), operated or owned by the government.

Patronage (political)

This refers to the use of state resources to reward individuals for their electoral or political support. What is legally accepted as political patronage differs by country and jurisdiction. It was traditional in Canada, for example, for the Prime Minister to appoint senators (recent amendments have modified this process). The Prime Minister still appoints people to head a number of commissions and agencies. It was (and, according to many critics, still is) common for many of these appointments go to people who have supported the political party of the Prime Minister.

Petition

A petition is a request to do something, most commonly addressed to a government official or public entity. In common parlance, a petition is a document addressed to some official and signed by numerous individuals.

Power Broker

This is a person who influences people to vote towards a particular client or agenda item in exchange for political and financial benefits. Power brokers can also negotiate deals with other power brokers to meet their aims. Power brokers often encapsulate the popular image of the "lobbyist".

Public Consultation

Public consultation, public comment, or simply consultation, pertains to a regulatory process by which the public's input on matters affecting them is sought. Its main goals are in improving the efficacy, efficiency, transparency and public involvement in laws, regulations and policies.

Public Policy

Public Policy generally denotes both the purpose of government action and the views on the best or preferred means of carrying it out; more specifically it refers to government actions designed to achieve one or more objectives (although considerable academic debate continues to centre around the definition of what public policy is and what it is not).

Public Sector

That part of the economy that is comprised of, and controlled by, the government, entailing both public services and public enterprises. See Para-Public Sector for comparison.

Public Servant (Civil Servant in some jurisdictions)

A public servant is generally a person who is employed by the government, including agencies, boards and commissions, whose institutional tenure typically survives transitions of political leadership or elections. Public servants are responsible to the elected government, not a political party. They develop and deliver public programs or services, inform policymaking, and provide evidence-based advice. Public servants exist at all levels of government.

Riding/Constituency/Electoral District

In Canada and the US, this is the geographical area that is represented by one Member of Parliament, Representative or Senator.

Royal Assent

The ceremony of Royal Assent is the last stage in the legislative process in the Westminster-styled legislature. Royal Assent takes place in the Senate Chamber and is given by the Governor General or the Governor General's deputy (the Chief Justice of Canada or another justice of the Supreme Court of Canada), with Members of the House of Commons present. Once a bill has received Royal Assent it can become law. Alternatively, Royal Assent may be signified by a written declaration by the Governor General or the Governor General's deputy.

Regulation

A Regulation is an official rule. Certain administrative agencies have a narrow authority to control conduct, within their areas of

11

responsibility (a Lobbying Register and Lobbying Commissioner, for example). These agencies have been delegated legislative power to create and apply the rules, or "regulations".

Speech from the Throne (British and British-styled parliamentary systems)

A speech prepared by the Privy Council Office and delivered by the Queen or the Governor General at the start of a session of Parliament. The speech is delivered in the Senate Chamber and outlines the Government's policies and the legislation (broadly speaking) it plans to introduce during the session.

State of the Union (US)

The State of the Union Address is an annual message delivered by the President of the United States to the US Congress near the beginning of each calendar year on the current condition of the nation. The message typically includes reports on the nation's budget, economy, news, agenda, achievements and the president's priorities and broad legislative proposals.

Talking Points

Talking points, also known as talking point memoranda, are re-established messaging (often featuring questions and answers as a central element) used in the field of political communication, sales and commercial or advertising communication. The message is designed to be invariable regardless of which stakeholder delivers the message.

HOW TO DEVELOP YOUR ADVOCACY CAMPAIGN

1. Set your Goal

- Specificity: Be specific about what you want to accomplish with your advocacy campaign;
- Measurability: Quantify your goal, which facilitates the tracking of progress and the confirmation of subsequent steps;
- Attainability: Focus on deliverables and what is do-able;
- Relevance: Define how the goal, and the objectives of that goal, will produce benefits (and to whom); and
- Timeliness: Deadlines also help define goals. Even ongoing advocacy will have points of achievement, and, quite often, beginnings and ends.

2. Identify your Target

Prior to any efforts designed to change policies or laws, it is vital to identify the people who are in a position to make that change. This is the target of your advocacy.

3. Build Your Team

Nearly every advocacy initiative or project requires more than one person. Advocacy teams include administration, content creation and promotion, sponsors, and volunteer/network/community engagement.

4. Define Your Message

Focus on crafting your messaging, which will be used to engage supporters and ultimately reach the campaign target. Part of defining the message is correctly defining the problem - the other key part of appreciating how a chosen solution relates to the problem.

5. Map a Timeline

Mapping requires realistic, not idealistic, considerations. Identify and factor-in internal and external considerations.

HOW TO PREPARE YOUR GOVERNMENT SUBMISSION AND PRESENT TO COMMITTEE

Individuals and groups can participate in committees at all levels of government. Committees are made up of small working groups of elected representatives. These committees consider specific issues that the elected assembly has tasked to review.

Participation can take several forms: appearing as a committee witness and making a presentation; submitting written material, such as a brief, to a committee; or attending committee hearings in-person.

Appear as a committee witness

The first step in appearing before a committee is informing the administrative contact for that committee that you and your organization would like to appear. This person is usually called a clerk. Some legislatures also have online applications for those wishing to appear as a committee witness. It is common for a "notice of hearing" to be posted on a legislature's website. In addition to contact information for you and the organization you represent, clerks will typically also require presenters' names and titles, as well as the name and number of the bill or issue in question. The clerk (or administrative coordinator for the committee) then contacts those witnesses who were chosen to appear.

Written submissions (discussed in the next section) are usually requested in advance of the date you are requested to appear. Typically, committee members will already have copies of your submission. However, it is wise to bring four to six extra copies. Even if committee members do not require them, the clerk or any media representatives in attendance might welcome a copy of your presentation.

Once you and your colleagues arrive at the legislature to appear before the committee on the day of your presentation, you'll want to remember that everything is recorded and will be made available on the permanent public record of the legislature. Your name and testimony will be published in the committee's transcripts. Your presentation may be recorded for broadcast or streamed as a webcast.

There is usually a time limit for each presentation, followed by a set number of questions from specific committee members. For this reason, do not reiterate the document you submit – since the committee already has it. Never consume your limited time and opportunity to read what committee members already have. State your name, organization and names of colleagues, and condense the highlights in order to stimulate questions and discussion.

- Include factual information to support your conclusions, views, or claims.
- Your recommendations should be as specific as possible.
- Begin with a summary of the main conclusions and recommendations.
- Maintain brevity, succinctness and cogency in your delivery.

Written Submissions and Briefs

A written submission (a brief) is an important way of having a say in the policy and political process. Unfortunately, too few organizations fully appreciate the value of committee work and of submitting a brief.

The question often posed to witnesses at committees is: "What is your single most important request or recommendation?" This question posed by members of a committee reflects the stark reality that, in many cases, you only get one "wish"; so choose wisely.

Too many organizations walk into a committee hearing with a "laundry list" of items. What is your specific goal? Are you recommending the implementation of a tax credit that recognizes out-of-pocket expenses of your volunteers; a request for funding to build 50 new beds in your hospital; or an amendment to the zoning regulations to change the flow of traffic around your health facility? Focus on one goal, and support that goal with substantive research and factual information.

Start with an executive summary. Consolidate your summary into one page that highlights the brief's important points. Make sure to highlight and clearly state your recommendation or request in the executive summary. Also add a point or two about the key benefits, not just to your organization, but to the local and broader community, as well as the cost-effectiveness and administrative efficiency the government might realize through by implementing your recommendation.

Following the title page there should be a brief blurb about your organization or cause, such as the history, membership, objectives, programs, services and accomplishments over the years.

Your main content tells the story and why your solution is critical. Address the problem. Describe the issues, barriers involved, and offer one or two practical, very do-able options.

Conclude the brief with one or two final statements, as well as a bibliography if suitable.

Formats vary by government, but a fairly standard format is as follows:

Documents should be formatted as follows:
- Type should be double-spaced;
- Paper should be 8.5" x 11";
- Pages should be numbered;
- Printing should be in black ink on white paper; and
- Document should include a title page.

Finally, clearly identify the name and address of the person or organization making the submission on the title page. And include information about memberships and objectives, if submitted by a group or organization.

POINTS OF INFLUENCE

There are several opportunities in most jurisdictions to participate in the legislative process, to help advance dialogue, and to potentially make an impact on the political or policy agenda.

If only one rule-of-thumb governs each of the following points of influence it is that *timing is everything*.

Government Budgets

The process of creating an annual budget for any government begins the day following the release of the current year's budget. While the budget process has an annual target, formulating budgets is ongoing. Invariably, once the preliminary departmental work is well underway, elected officials and entire committees often reach out to constituents for feedback and recommendations.

Such outreach can take the simple form of media advertisements that ask individuals and groups to submit their own recommendations. Online polls are sometimes used, and usually feature a determined set of choices that people can rank in order of priority.

Outreach can also be more formal, entailing in-person dialogue and interaction. During a budget-making process, individual representatives may host local town-halls (open and invite-only), which are excellent vehicles for receiving feedback and recommendations on the government's spending priorities for the coming year. Budget-related committees (finance, ways and means) also publicize their meeting schedules, typically inviting individuals and organizations to (i) prepare and submit written papers and (ii) appear before committee members to present their information and respond to questions. The latter is sometimes broadcast or webcast, and is almost always recorded for the public and legislative record.

A local town-hall or a participation in a committee afford excellent opportunity for an organization to elevate awareness of an issue, as well as to heighten the official dialogue around possible solutions and changes to public policy.

Media are sometimes present in such gatherings, and representatives thereof may seek out interviews with presenters - an ideal opportunity to advance dialogue and elevate attention.

The content and results of such meetings and presentations can also be repurposed as communications pieces and narratives to be share with your organization's donors, shareholders, members and supporters. Remember to take photos if the committee allows.

The pre-budget process is only part of the participatory phase. Budget Day is the day when the budget is officially released. This annual event may offer individuals an opportunity to participate in "lock-ups". A budget lock-up is an assembly of interested parties (typically other advocacy and government relations specialists, as well as formal lobbyists, and media representatives), who gather in a room that is literally locked until the details of the government budget are made public. Participants who are granted access are able to interact with key political and government representatives, as well as counterparts representing other organizations or advocacy/lobby firms, and receive privileged details about the government budget hours prior to the budget's official release in the public realm. Since the information shared is sensitive to market fluctuations, participants in a lock-up are locked in those briefing rooms until the budget is officially made available to the public.

Not only do Budget Day exercises offer valuable avenues for networking, they can also open opportunity to engage with media, who might be covering an organization's issue and soliciting official commentary and feedback.

These sessions can also be repurposed in company newsletters, direct communication to members and supporters, as well as information update sessions on YouTube or through a special podcast.

Events

Special events can be many things: a town-hall hosted by the organization, featuring a live or recorded Q&A session; an annual general meeting; an awards ceremony; or a fundraising gala. The key opportunity associated with each type of event is the use of elected representatives, local and cabinet-defined, as a central feature in the event. That individual may offer welcoming remarks, deliver a keynote speech, or participate in a meet-and-greet with attendees. Such events, particularly if well-attended by cross-sections of professionals and or constituents, can be particularly attractive for elected representatives to attend. As with other points of influence, consult your local and national regulatory framework for lobbying and compliance to ensure that your form of participation and style of interaction with elected representatives do not break any rules.

Legislative Committees

Presentations and deputations, when and where available (government practices vary by jurisdiction), afford the opportunity to appear before a committee composed of members of the elected assembly and to formally respond to a specific bill. Getting on the "committee circuit" helps advance name and brand recognition, reinforce a reciprocal relationship between your organization (producing valuable input) and the policy maker, and can increase the likelihood of a particular recommendation being adopted by the committee - thereby making a change to part of a bill. See the earlier section, "How to Prepare a Government Submission", for details and guidance on requirements for process and format.

As with other appearances and forms of participation, narratives around such content can be repurposed in multiple ways.

Advocacy Days/Legislative Receptions

This vehicle for interaction, as a point of influence, is discussed in detail in the section, "Hosting a Reception".

Suffice at this point to identify the importance of advocacy days/legislative receptions. Instead of advocating outside the centre of power, advocacy days and legislative receptions move the practice inside the epicentre of legislative power.

Specific features of these vehicles include meetings with multiple representatives and public office holders, informal receptions that encourage one-on-one conversation and learning, and education sessions.

Assembling people for an advocacy day or a legislative reception is no simple task; but when coordinated effectively, the benefits are multiple: there are few other opportunities to meet with as many elected officials and public office holders in one place in such a short span of time; the interaction can often assume a more personal, "tell me more" type of tone; the creation of relationships; the identification of issue champions, who can then help advance the issue on their own behalf; and the reinforcement of one's community of supporters and members, who each experience and enjoy such benefits.

Statements by Members

The agenda in many legislatures includes a special amount of time allotted for elected representatives to speak about an issue or cause, or an organization or event, in their electoral district. For example, according to the Parliament of Canada (parl.gc.ca):

Members of Parliament represent their constituents in many ways; for example, by representing their views in the House of Commons and suggesting policy initiatives on their behalf. By partaking in the legislative process, MPs give constituents at least an indirect role in the shaping of important policies affecting their lives. A Member may make a short statement on any topic under Standing Order 31 immediately prior to the start of the daily oral Question Period. MPs may also raise matters during Question Period in the hope of influencing a Minister to alter or initiate policies more in keeping with the views of voters. Members may also appeal to Ministers either by letter or more directly.

Determine which member or representative represents the constituency in which your company or organization is located. The goal is to work with a representative's offices and aides to produce a short (one to two minutes) statement about your organization, its work, its mission and history, and value to the constituency. Once formulated and accepted into the legislature's agenda for the day, the statement can be officially read aloud by that representative. Aside from the permanent record that archives the statement, its main value is in content repurposing for such things as newsletters and other communication to members and supporters, social media content, and YouTube and podcast episodes (the video and audio of which may be requested from an officer of the legislative assembly in question; there is usually an audio/video production centre located in a legislative building).

Other systems, such as the congressional system in the US, allow for statements by Representatives and Senators in similar ways.

Debates

Some organizations use debate models as a point of influence. Typically, such debates are coordinated during the electoral period, featuring a panel of candidates competing for office. Such debates can focus on issues such as seniors, crime, healthcare, or inclusion, and can represent a way to elevate issues in public settings that potentially attract media attention, as well as putting views and positions of candidates "on the record".

The debate model, as a point of influence, is also useful during a governing term. For example, representatives from different political parties in the legislature, or representing different views about governance, could be invited to a webcast discussion that focuses on issues central to a particular organization (or group of organizations), thereby penetrating the online and digital world of consumption, and elevating the issues embraced by the organizing organizations.

Individual Meetings

The simplest, though sometimes more time-consuming, approach to exerting influence is a meeting with one, two or multiple representatives in that individual's office. A simple email or phone call, with some written explanatory material, is usually sufficient to book a meeting to secure face-time with elected representatives. As with other points of influence, consult your local, regional and national rules on lobbying and advocacy as regards your type of organization and the purpose of the meeting you hope to arrange.

Which brings us to the next point of influence: specialized forms of outreach.

Summer Outreach Initiatives

Summer can be a time when many elected representatives are not in their offices as frequently as, say, during a formal legislative session. It is a time when students and other volunteers may be more readily available and enthusiastic about participating in your advocacy cause. Continued outreach during these slower months also maintains consistency of the advocacy efforts.

Summer outreach, however, should be customized for something softer, something more practical. Remembering that nurturing a reciprocal relationship is a constant goal, a summer outreach campaign can focus on providing constituency offices, for example, with information and tips. Consider the following scenario: an organization is committed to having new building code measures implemented to help advance physical accessibility for mobility-limited seniors. During the "off" months, the organization requires a different point of influence, since the committees, advocacy days or other points of influence are not available for that time in the governing calendar. The advocacy team still wants to reinforce brand awareness, continue nurturing reciprocal relations, and reinforce previous efforts of advancing the issue or cause. So the advocacy team targets the community and constituency offices of elected representatives, which, during the summer months, are staffed by a greater extent with students and volunteers, rather than professional aides and policy experts. The advocacy team, either in-person or through conventional mail, sends a customized "tip card" that features advice on how to easily and inexpensively make the constituency offices more accessible and welcoming to seniors with limited mobility. With accompanying organization information and contact details, that card becomes a useful tool for anyone in the constituency office, and one that has considerable shelf life.

Summer outreach initiatives really are creative opportunities. Keep in mind, though, that such exercises must be considered useful by the individuals receiving the information. Points of influence need not be formulaic and necessarily tied only to a legislature's agenda. A bit of creativity, and a healthy respect for information that is mutually useful (as opposed to gimmicky), can open yet another opportunity for a point of influence that is often overlooked.

Take-Away Advice

In any point of influence, there are 50 other individuals pulling for the attention and time of the elected representative. Recognize this fact, and that your cause and your organization reside in an ocean of advocacy (which also includes higher-powered corporate lobbyists). Keep your points clear, concise and succinct. A legislator will respect you and your issue more if you respect their time and schedule.

In all communication, include: the name and number of the bill in question (or the name of the rule or regulation); your organization's complete contact information, including a simple and fast way to contact one point-person; and the three to five key points about your issue, such as number of people affected.

Always try to be helpful. Don't be afraid to ask about including any additional information and data that might lead to more persuasive communication. You're asking for the assistance vis-a-vis support from the elected representative; ask that representative if there is anything more you can do to help advance and assist their efforts.

Constantly compile, and confirm the accuracy of, lists of contact information for all legislators. Also do research to find out how to receive automated updates from the outreach and distribution lists of government departments or agencies.

Constantly think about larger impacts of your advocacy and lobbying. What is the estimated reach, both direct and indirect? This is the "wow" data that public officer holders need. Remember that public policy not only must include the public, but its impact is on the public. So attempt to maintain a keen grasp on just how much of an impact your changes on public policy will make.

Determine what is do-able, that item which can be implemented with the proverbial stroke of a pen, compared with those outcomes that will take months and years to achieve.

Remember that you are the expert in your issue. Part of your role will be education and information sharing. Avoid sector-based lingo and buzzwords, and never assume that the public official knows the issue to the extent that you do.

Regularly share information updates from and about your organization with the public office holders within your realm of capture. Whether those updates are newsletters or annual reports, share them with your contact list. Most importantly, for those names in the centre of your focus, add personal notes that highlight specific information relevant to that recipient. Enhance the usefulness of the information, and, in so doing, confirm the value of your organization and its advocacy goals.

HOSTING A RECEPTION, ADVOCACY DAY, OR INFORMATION SESSION

Why Consider Coordinating a Special Day?

Advocacy efforts are typically coordinated from one's corporate headquarters or place of small business. Even if the work is contracted out, that work is based in an office separate from members, supporters, partners and, most importantly, public officials.

Special days have the potential of assembling all parties into one space. While there are tremendous benefits derived from digital and online innovations in the world of advocacy, none of these benefits outweighs the importance of in-person meetings and face-to-face interaction.

Some people refer to these events as "advocacy days", others call them "lobby days", and some refer to them as "legislative days" ("day of action" has even popped up once or twice). Regardless of the choice of terminology, these special days involve a reception of some sort, plenty of advocacy work and the sharing and exchange of information.

The day is designed to entail multiple brief meetings with legislators and other public office holders that explain your organization, communicate your cause or issue, and focus on the changes to laws or policies that need to be made. The day also illustrates the breadth and depth of your supporters, members, donors and partners.

If coordinated effectively, special days can generate more meetings and more interaction with a greater number of relevant individuals than most other advocacy efforts.

Special days represent important opportunities to network with members of your larger community. They also present a unique point of influence in the legislative process, with the benefit of meeting with many elected officials on a personal basis.

While many of the people you hope to meet likely work in or very near the legislative building in which your special day will be coordinated, all those others from your community - volunteers, staff, members, supporters, donors, shareholders, partner groups, and media (internal social media and external traditional media representatives), have to physically arrive at the location. Interestingly, one of the draws (and, sometimes a point that impresses at least a few people) is the building itself, sometimes its history and architecture, what it represents and who is based there. Not only does the event location sometimes encourage momentum among members of your community, many people have never been inside the main legislative building in their locality. There is a certain appeal and novelty to hosting your efforts in such a location.

What about Virtual Special Days?

The reality of meetings and special events since late 2019 and early 2020 is that virtual organizing is not only possible, but sometimes necessary. If this approach is the only viable option, then proceed with assembling your participants and attendees via Zoom (as one example). There are certain advantages to virtual special days, including lower costs (for example, food, travel and parking, or hotel accommodation). Furthermore, there are some attendees who might prefer to participate via virtual conferencing due to difficulty travelling or day-to-day mobility restrictions. Another benefit to virtual special days, one that is related to the relative ease of coordinating multiple participants via Zoom as well as the reduced costs, may be found in the opportunity to organize more than one special virtual day. For example, your organization may want its national focus for a special day based somewhere in DC or Ottawa. You might also want to organize subnational events where strategic opportunities warrant, perhaps in legislative buildings in Halifax or Sacramento. Virtual is never a replacement for in-person, but it can offer unique benefits.

Organizing any special event can seem like an insurmountable task, leaving many people asking, "Where do I start?"

Know Your Issue and the Message: Simple, Quick and To-The-Point

Focus on one to three points to share with legislators. Do not attempt to advance a "laundry list" comprised of multiple items. If you can't encapsulate your message and goal into the space of a lapel button, odds are you are still somewhat hazy on the message.

Identify Do-Able Goals

You will not achieve a 100% level of turnout among legislators and public office holders. By many estimates, a 20% turnout is considered high. Expectations of total, or near total, turnout are unrealistic.

Also know that the special day you are organizing is not an outcome, but one of many steps in the advocacy process. Goals at this point should focus on education, expressions of interest and commitment, breadth of message distribution, or number of requests generated (for example, requests for more information or another meeting).

Do not expect attendance by, or meetings solely with, elected officials. Staffers and aides are experts in their own right (in some cases, far more so than the elected representative), and many are public office holders "in waiting". Welcome elected officials as well as their legislative, policy and political staff.

Three Main Components: Direct Advocacy, Reception and Information Session

Typically, a special day features an information session for all members of your community (an orientation of sorts); multiple meetings with elected representatives or the aides thereof; and a reception that is more informal in nature.

Ideally, someone is assigned to coordinating meetings. Another person is responsible for the information session. A third crafts the agenda and plan for a reception.

What Steps are involved?

Review the legislative calendar in an effort to determine the level and volume of "traffic" on a given day. Ideally, your day won't compete with similar efforts by other advocacy groups. You also want to ensure that elected representatives are not in their constituencies on that day.

Send a "save the date" email 60 to 90 days ahead of the event (this is followed by firm invitations that provide more event details).

Timing is critical. An ideal time for a reception, for example, is around 7am or 4pm.

In some jurisdictions, the use of event rooms in the legislative building may require a "sponsor", which is essentially an endorsement by an elected member of the legislature confirming the use of the building's facilities. The event is usually hosted in that person's name (which can have its own advantages as regards distribution of information, invitations and related material).

Begin personal outreach (phone or email) to confirm in-person meetings.
Maintain a document that logs all interaction with each office.

Send a second invitation to those who have not replied.

Coordinate with the Speaker's office to have a printed flyer placed in each member's mail on the day of the event.

If you are working with a "sponsor" ask that individual to help promote the event. If a sponsor is not required, a representative who expresses enthusiasm might be a suitable person to make such an appeal to colleagues.

The point-person for your reception will need to consider event logistics, such as cocktails, coffee and food. Late afternoon receptions represent a perfect time for representatives or staff to visit your reception, have a cocktail, and mingle with your community. An early morning event focuses more on juices, coffee or small breakfast items that equally facilitate mingling and networking.

Coordinating Your Community

Your community can consist of staff in your organization, counterparts in the industry or sector, members, shareholders, supporters, donors, partners and volunteers. Early estimates of attendance are necessary for access to the premises. Security will likely need a list of all names. Additionally, most legislatures now require security screening for access, and the issuance of temporary passes. Depending on the numbers of attendees, this process can be time-consuming.

Assemble and distribute (in advance, if possible) kits for each member of your community in attendance that day. Kits should include: an agenda for the day; talking points with questions and answers; clear and concise policy positions that your organization is advocating; information sheets that can be left behind at meetings or handed out to anyone interested; and a map of the legislative building, indicating main entrances, washrooms, and nearby parking and transit access.

Volunteers are critical to successfully executing a special day. Carefully gauge the number of volunteers needed. Everything from phone calls, preparation of material, and assembly of kits, to coordinating and logging appointments, requires help.

Additional considerations for event volunteers: a welcoming coordinator for community members (all attendees); someone to distribute kits and other material; a point-person (or two) to welcome elected representatives and/or their staff, as well as someone to make introductions to other guests; someone to handle logistics (for example, coordinating technical/audio/video requirements; building, internal services and facilities management; catering); people who will lead the information session (orientation activist); one or two people handling social media, photography, webcasting, audio recording or traditional media; and someone (likely one of the media coordinators) who can encourage legislative or political staff to share content in their newsletters and social media feeds.

The Importance of Follow-Up in the Advocacy Trajectory

Once the special day, the event itself, is complete, one should remember to actively follow-up on each component of the event as it relates to the current status of your advocacy efforts and the policy or political goals you have identified.

One simple, but very important, way to do this is by thanking those who attended your reception, as well as thanking the staff and representatives with whom you met. Try to add useful information in your follow-up.

Did anyone request additional information? Make sure they get it. Did anyone express interest in visiting your offices to meet with other staff or to personally tour your company's operations? Reach out to that person and book the time.

Follow up with partners, supporters or anyone else who is significant on an operation level. Your conversation with this group should ask questions like: Were we successful? How do we know? What could have been done better or more effectively? Where can we go next? What works best for everyone involved? What changes would we make for a future special day?

Another piece of follow-up may entail the preparation of an accountability report, whether to your organization's "top brass" or to your client.

Of course, you'll want to log and organize all content captured during the special day. This content might include such things as audio recording of a speech; video recording of a presentation; photos from the reception or from individual meetings. This type of content is perfectly suited for repurposing during the advocacy campaign through vehicles like newsletters, social media posts or podcasts and YouTube updates.

Finally, as any astute reader will surmise, you will need to extract key information from all points of the special day that were diarized for the purposes of filing an activity report with your lobbying compliance office of relevance. Even if your jurisdiction exempts you or your organization from registering and filing as a lobbyist, you have, nonetheless, engaged in direct, coordinated advocacy activity that has a goal of somehow changing a public policy, rule, regulation or law. The maintenance of such information, even if filing is not required, can serve as useful planning data for future events and other special days.

FAQs

Do the disclosure and transparency requirements in lobbying legislative frameworks mean that people can no longer just pick up the phone, have a direct conversation with an elected representative, and put an idea into action?

Not at all. The rules for reporting lobbying activity simply mean that, prior to picking up that telephone, one must be registered with a lobbying authority, and later report to that authority the event of that conversation as well as other details (the depth of which varies from jurisdiction to jurisdiction), usually including the purpose of the call, dates and times, names and organizations of other participants, and outcomes achieved. A publicly-accountable paper trail now accompanies interaction and dialogue. So, provided the prescribed requirements are met, anyone can still "pick up the phone"; knowing, however, that the activity report of that phone call may later be scrutinized by anyone who chooses to read the report filed with the lobbying authority.

Is it considered acceptable for staff in my organization to interact with public office holders, especially when those staff persons claim to personally know the official in question?

While this is not to be considered as legal advice (as nothing in this handbook should), it is best to exercise an abundance of caution in all advocacy efforts. As there is such a variance in what is captured in lobbying legislation versus what is exempt, it is wise to implement a system that emphasizes zero-tolerance for staff who reach out to government or political contacts. Everyone claims to know someone important, and herein lies a potential pitfall: even a staff member in a charitable NGO might know the mayor of his town from childhood years, but it is no less a breach of lobbying rules in some jurisdictions for that individual to contact that mayor on questions related to funding applications - without at least recording an itemization of all details related to the communication. While your organization might be exempt from registering and filing, your exemption could possibly disappear with a legislative refinement of lobbying rules in the next fiscal year. You are nonetheless engaged in advocating for change that impacts policy or political systems, and that alone should emphasize cautionary due diligence.

What are the consequences for failing to register my lobbying undertakings?

Penalties across jurisdictions range from fines to administrative and criminal penalties. For example, the Government of Canada's website informs of the following: *There are consequences for not complying with the provisions of the Lobbying Act and the Lobbyists' Code of Conduct. The Act provides for penalties for lobbyists who are found guilty of failing to register or making false or misleading statements in any return or document submitted to the Lobbying Commissioner and are liable: on summary conviction, to a fine not exceeding $50,000 or to imprisonment for a term not exceeding six months, or to both; and on proceedings by way of indictment, to a fine not exceeding $200,000 or to imprisonment for a term not exceeding two years, or to both. The Lobbying Commissioner may also impose a prohibition on lobbying for up to two years on anyone convicted under the Act. If an individual breaches a principle or a rule of the Code, the Commissioner will make this public in a Report on Investigation tabled in both Houses of Parliament.* Source: (lobbyingcanada.gc.ca)

Are petitions useful?

Petitions can be highly effective if used correctly and judiciously. The cautionary note highlights the fact that petitions are not, and should not be viewed, as the go-to tool in advocacy. They have a purpose, both inside and outside legislative assemblies, in advancing an issue and demonstrating levels of citizen support. However, petitions are often misused and frequently misunderstood as tools for effecting change to public policy. More detailed discussion of petitions may be found in Chapter 5, "Methods and Techniques", from the larger book, *Advocacy: Explained!*

Is it still called advocacy if my organization is invited to make a presentation and appear before a government committee considering budgetary priorities?

It is advocacy, but might not constitute the legal definition of lobbying See below.

Does someone have to register as a lobbyist if that person is participating in a government-initiated consultation?

The breadth of capture by lobbying definitions and frameworks excludes government-initiated consultation in some places and fully includes all consultation in others. In Canada, at the national level, for example, the application of compliance is conditional: If the meeting is closed, with no public record of participants, registration and filing is likely necessary. In cases where the communications take place in an open forum, and the names and statements of participants are a matter of public record, registration would not be required. For example, parliamentary committees are transparent in terms of participants, proceedings, and decisions. Conversely, closed meetings involving unknown participants, with no record of discussions or decisions, and no details about the proceedings, are less transparent (if at all). Thus, as a consultation process approaches the transparency level of a parliamentary committee, the requirement for registration becomes less necessary. (Source: lobbycanada.gc.ca) Bottom line: consult the government of relevance in your jurisdiction of activity, as requirements and legislative capture vary considerably.

Are non-profit organizations allowed to lobby?

Non-profit and charitable organizations can lobby. In the US, for example, the key is to make sure that the lobbying remains at a level that is acceptable to the Internal Revenue Service (IRS). Section 501(c)(3) states that US non-profits are allowed to engage in some lobbying without losing their tax-exempt status. Bottom line: make sure the efforts remain at a level that are acceptable to the IRS.

The situation in Canada is characterized by "ifs", "ands" and "buts" (which is by no means a negative characterization of Canada's lobbying framework), as well as conflict of interest rules that govern the conduct of elected representatives at the federal level. For example, a non-profit that submits a bid or application for a grant is not considered lobbying. However, it is lobbying if a representative of that organization sets up a meeting outside the bidding process in an attempt to influence the outcome of the bid. If contact between the public office holder and the organization in question is initiated by the public office holder, that interaction is not considered as lobbying in some (but not all) provinces. However, on "prescribed" subjects, any "paid" communication with a public office holder is considered lobbying, regardless of which party initiated the contact. Grassroots lobbying can be covered by Canadian lobbying legislation. For example, the definition of lobbying is applied should a representative of an organization persuade members of the public to communicate directly with a public office holder in an attempt to pressure the public office holder to endorse a particular policy position or opinion. Bottom line: if you, or your organization, ask members of the public to contact their elected Members of Parliament about a cause or issue, you may have fallen under the capture of lobbying legislation.

There is further distinction between non-profit organizations generally and those non-profits which operate with charitable status (in other words, those that can issue tax receipts for donations). Should a charitable representative "communicate with a public officer holder" asking for funds, that action is likely viewed as "lobbying" - if that representative's time dedicated to such activity constitutes more than 20% of a full-time equivalent over any given month. This references the "significant part of duties" rule (hence, the "ifs", "ands" or "buts").

The definition of "communication" in Canada's lobbying legislation as regards charities includes verbal or written contact with a public office holder.

Office of the Commissioner   Commissariat au lobbying
of Lobbying of Canada   du Canada

CANADA'S LOBBYISTS' CODE OF CONDUCT

Preamble

The Lobbying Act is based on four principles:
- Free and open access to government is an important matter of public interest;
- Lobbying public office holders is a legitimate activity;
- It is desirable that public office holders and the public be able to know who is engaged in lobbying activities; and
- A system for the registration of paid lobbyists should not impede free and open access to government.

The Lobbying Act provides the Commissioner with the authority to develop and administer a code of conduct for lobbyists. The Commissioner has done so, with these four principles in mind. The Lobbyists' Code of Conduct is an important instrument for promoting public trust in the integrity of government decision making. The trust that Canadians place in public office holders to make decisions in the public interest is vital to a free and democratic society.

Public office holders, when they deal with the public and with lobbyists, are required to adhere to the standards set out for them in their own codes of conduct. For their part, lobbyists communicating with public office holders must also abide by standards of conduct, which are set out below.

These codes complement one another and together contribute to public confidence in the integrity of government decision-making. *Principles*

- Respect for democratic institutions.
- Lobbyists should act in a manner that demonstrates respect for democratic institutions, including the duty of public office holders to serve the public interest.

Integrity and honesty

Lobbyists should conduct with integrity and honesty all relations with public office holders.

Openness

Lobbyists should be open and frank about their lobbying activities.

Professionalism

Lobbyists should observe the highest professional and ethical standards. In particular, lobbyists should conform fully with the letter and the spirit of the Lobbyists' Code of Conduct as well as with all relevant laws, including the Lobbying Act and its regulations.

Rules

Transparency, identity and purpose

A lobbyist shall, when communicating with a public office holder, disclose the identity of the person, organization or corporation on whose behalf the communication is made and the nature of their relationship with that person, organization or corporation, as well as the reasons for the approach.

Accurate information

A lobbyist shall avoid misleading public office holders by taking all reasonable measures to provide them with information that is accurate and factual.

Duty to disclose

A consultant lobbyist shall inform each client of their obligations as a lobbyist under the Lobbying Act and the Lobbyists' Code of Conduct.

The responsible officer (the most senior paid employee) of an organization or corporation shall ensure that employees who lobby on the organization's or corporation's behalf are informed of their obligations under the Lobbying Act and the Lobbyists' Code of Conduct.

Use of information

A lobbyist shall use and disclose information received from a public office holder only in the manner consistent with the purpose for which it was shared. If a lobbyist obtains a government document they should not have, they shall neither use nor disclose it.

Conflict of interest

A lobbyist shall not propose or undertake any action that would place a public office holder in a real or apparent conflict of interest.

Specifics

Preferential access

A lobbyist shall not arrange for another person a meeting with a public office holder when the lobbyist and public office holder share a relationship that could reasonably be seen to create a sense of obligation. A lobbyist shall not lobby a public office holder with whom they share a relationship that could reasonably be seen to create a sense of obligation.

Political activities

When a lobbyist undertakes political activities on behalf of a person which could reasonably be seen to create a sense of obligation, they may not lobby that person for a specified period if that person is or becomes a public office holder. If that person is an elected official, the lobbyist shall also not lobby staff in their office(s).

Gifts

To avoid the creation of a sense of obligation, a lobbyist shall not provide or promise a gift, favour, or other benefit to a public office holder, whom they are lobbying or will lobby, which the public office holder is not allowed to accept.

Source: lobbycanada.gc.ca

UNITED STATES CODE OF ETHICS, NATIONAL ASSOCIATION OF STATE LOBBYISTS

NASL

NATIONAL ASSOCIATION
of
STATE LOBBYISTS

We believe that a lobbyist:

- Should comply with all federal and state laws, regulations and local ordinances that apply to lobbying and related government affairs activities.

- Should never cause or encourage any public official, policymaker or other person to violate any law or rule applicable to them.

- Should not facilitate or otherwise participate in an apparent violation.

- Should not bring discredit to the profession, to government or to colleagues by their conduct.

- Should always conduct themselves and the representation of their clients to protect their clients from any scandal or violation.

WE KNOW THAT INTEGRITY IS A LOBBYIST'S MOST IMPORTANT PRODUCT, AND NOT TO BE COMPROMISED, NOR SUBJECT TO CONFLICTS.

We believe that a lobbyist:

- Should strive to maintain professional relationships based upon honesty and integrity.

- Should not undertake or continue representations that create, or are likely to create, conflicts of interest in the absence of the knowledgeable consent of the clients involved.

- Should not advocate on behalf of one client if the lobbyist also represents another client with an adverse position without the consent of both clients.

- Should affirmatively, fully and timely disclose a potential conflict to a client and resolve it in a manner that is clearly understood and acceptable to the client, or otherwise withdraw from the conflicting representation.

WE CONSIDER TRUSTWORTHINESS AND CREDIBILITY OUR MOST IMPORTANT GOALS, AND HONEST AND ACCURATE INFORMATION OUR MOST IMPORTANT TOOLS.

We believe that a lobbyist:
- Should provide accurate, current and factual information, whether it is being reported to his or her employer or client, government officials, the media or professional colleagues.
- Should not engage in any misrepresentations. Should accurately represent the client's positions and policies.
- Should promptly correct any inaccurate information provided or submissions later determined to be in need of correction, and should update information provided as necessary to keep it from being misleading.

WE BELIEVE IN THE REPRESENTATIVE SYSTEM OF GOVERNMENT AND ITS PROCESSES, AND THAT ITS STRENGTH IS BASED IN INFORMED DECISION MAKERS AND FAIR PARTICIPATION BY ALL INTERESTED PARTIES AND OPPONENTS.

We believe that a lobbyist:
- Should always seek to strengthen and protect the integrity of the public policy process.
- Should serve as a source of reliable information, using their expertise and awareness to explain and assist in the understanding of the varied aspects of complex public issues.

- Should at all times exhibit the proper respect for our democratic institutions and processes, public officials and policymakers, and fellow government affairs professionals.
- Should not act in any manner that will undermine public confidence and trust in the governmental process.
- Should recognize and encourage diverse viewpoints within the public policy process, acknowledging that disagreement on issues is both inevitable and healthy.
- Should recognize that informed decisions are the best and should assist in ensuring that decision makers have balanced information on both sides of the issue.

AS LEADERS IN OUR PROFESSION, WE ARE PROUD OF IT AND TAKE EVERY OPPORTUNITY TO ENSURE THAT OTHERS UNDERSTAND ITS VALUE IN THE PROCESS, OUR STANDARDS OF INTEGRITY, AND OUR PROUD ROLE.

We believe that a lobbyist:
- Should uphold the dignity and standards of the government affairs profession by counseling or even admonishing those government affairs colleagues who manifest behaviors that are inconsistent with these lobbying principles.
- Should publicly acknowledge his or her role as a legitimate participant in the public policy process, and the right of every interested participant to present their information and utilize lobbyists to do so. Should take every opportunity to increase the understanding of our true role and standards of integrity and trust, and our value as advocates in informing the process and the decisions it makes.

CONFIDENTIALITY IS A TRADEMARK OF OUR PROFESSION, WHICH WE GUARD CAREFULLY.

We believe that a lobbyist:

- Should always protect confidences, not only those of employers or clients but those of elected and appointed officials of government and colleagues.

WE ARE STRONG PROPONENTS OF DISCLOSURE AND REPORTING OF RELATIONSHIPS, CONTRIBUTIONS, GIFTS AND OTHER RELEVANT INFORMATION BEARING ON THE OPENNESS AND HONESTY OF THE PROCESS.

We believe that a lobbyist:

- Should support and honor full disclosure, recordkeeping and reporting as required by law.
- Should encourage full reporting and disclosure by others in the process, and erring on the side of full disclosure when there is any question.

AS LEADERS IN OUR PROFESSION, WE RECOGNIZE OUR ROLE IN KEEPING THE STANDARDS OF THE PROFESSION HIGH AND IN INFLUENCING OUR FELLOW PROFESSIONALS TO DO THE SAME.

We believe that a lobbyist:

- Should conduct their relationships with fellow government affairs professionals with the highest standards of fairness, dignity and respect.
- Should not solicit or knowingly permit solicitation of a prospective client for the purpose of obtaining professional employment if the member knows or reasonably should know that the client to whom the solicitation is directed is already represented by a government affairs professional in the matter.

THE SUCCESS OF THE CLIENT IS PARAMOUNT TO US, AS IS THEIR COMPLETE PARTICIPATION AND COMMUNICATION IN OUR EFFORTS AND STRATEGIES.

We believe that a lobbyist:
- Should keep a client fully informed as to relevant events relating to the client.
- Should give the client meaningful and informed participation in the development and implementation of strategies and the prioritization of the acceptability of potential results.
- Should maintain the confidentiality of information provided by the client and of any other confidential information that would be contrary to the client's material interests if disclosed.
- Should have a written agreement with the client regarding the engagement with the client that clearly defines the relationship and services to be provided, including the amount and terms of compensation.
- Should conduct the representation of clients diligently and vigorously to advance the interest of the client.
- Should devote the necessary time, attention and resources to the interests of the client. Should always emphasize how the client's interests align with the public interest.

AS EXPERTS IN THE STATE LEGISLATIVE AND POLITICAL PROCESSES, WE PRIDE OURSELVES ON BEING THE BEST INFORMED AND MOST COMPETENT.

We believe that a lobbyist:
- Should fully understand the legislative, governmental and political processes in order to represent a client or an employer in the most competent and effective manner.
- Should be current in the ethical, campaign and election laws and restrictions, and other areas affecting the respect and reputation of the profession.

- Should maintain a high level of current knowledge of relevant specialized subject areas to ensure the ability to be an effective participant in all major policy issues.

- Should participate in continuing education, seminars and similar activities to maintain a current and ongoing high level of proficiency.

Source: www.statelobbyists.org/code-of-ethics/

LOBBYING LEGISLATION RULES IN CANADA

The following is directly referenced from the Government of Canada. Sub-national lobbying registration also exists in Canada, for example at the provincial, territorial and municipal levels, the details of which are available online.

The Lobbying Act and its related Regulations came into force simultaneously on July 2, 2008. The Lobbying Act is based on four key principles:

- Free and open access to government is an important matter of public interest;
- Lobbying public office holders is a legitimate activity;
- It is desirable that public office holders and the general public be able to know who is engaged in lobbying activities; and
- The system of registration of paid lobbyists should not impede free and open access to government.

The Act applies to individuals who are paid to lobby. People who lobby on a voluntary basis are not required to register.

The Lobbyists' Code of Conduct

The Commissioner of Lobbying has the authority to develop, administer and enforce a Lobbyists' Code of Conduct. The purpose of the Code is to assure Canadians that lobbying is done ethically and in accordance with the highest standards. Lobbyists are required to comply with the Code.

What is lobbying?

Three elements define lobbying:

1. The individual is paid by an employer or a client;
2. The individual communicates directly (i.e. either in writing or orally) or indirectly (i.e. grassroots communication), with a federal public office holder; and
3. The individual communicates about one of the following subjects:
    - Development of any legislative proposal;
    - Introduction, defeat or amendment of any Bill or resolution;
    - Making or amendment of any regulation;
    - Development or amendment of any policy or program;
    - Awarding of any grant, contribution or other financial benefit; and
    - Awarding of any contract (Consultant lobbyists only)

OR

    - The individual arranges a meeting between a public office holder and any other person (Consultant lobbyists only).

What is not lobbying?

The following types of oral or written communications are not registrable lobbying activities:
- submissions to Parliamentary Committees;
- communications with a public office holder concerning the enforcement; interpretation or the application of any Act of Parliament or regulation; and
- communications made to a public office holder that are limited to a request for information.

What type of lobbyist are you?

In-House lobbyist

Employee of a corporation or an organization who communicates with public office holders on behalf of their employer.

The most senior paid employee is responsible for filing a registration for a corporation or organization.

Registration is required within two months of when lobbying activities constitute a significant part of the duties of one full-time employee.

Consultant lobbyist

An individual who communicates with a federal public office holder, for payment, on behalf of a client (i.e. another individual, a company or an organization).

An individual who arranges a meeting between a public office holder and any other person.

Consultant lobbyists are required to register each of their lobbying undertakings no later than 10 days after entering into an undertaking.

Federal Designated Public Office Holders (DPOHs) are:
- All MPs and Senators;
- Ministers and their exempt staff;
- Some staff in the Office of the Leader of the Opposition;
- Deputy Ministers;
- Associate and Assistant Deputy Ministers, and those of comparable rank (Interpretation bulletin on Comparable Rank);
- 7 senior positions in the Armed Forces;
- Comptroller General of Canada; and
- Select positions at the Privy Council Office.

What is a significant part of duties?

The most senior paid officer must file a return when one or more employees communicate with public office holders on registrable topics on behalf of the employer, and the cumulative lobbying activities of all employees constitutes a "Significant Part of Duties," interpreted as 20% or more of one person's time over a one-month period. Time spent by all employees preparing for communicating, e.g. (research, writing, planning, travelling, etc.) and actually communicating with public office holders should be considered.

In situations where the time related to lobbying is difficult to estimate, the officer responsible for filing will have to estimate the relative importance of the lobbying activities. Both methods may be used in conjunction if the situation is unclear. The officer responsible for filing is accountable for the decision as to whether or not a registration is necessary.

Source: lobbycanada.gc.ca

GOVERNMENT LINKS FOR LOBBYING IN CANADA

Federal

Office of the Commissioner of Lobbying
of Canada
410 Laurier Avenue West, 8th floor
Ottawa, Ontario K1R 1B7
613-957-2760

https://lobbycanada.gc.ca/

Federal Lobbyists Registration System:
https://lobbycanada.gc.ca/app/secure/ocl/lrs/do/guest

The Lobbying Act of Canada:
https://lobbycanada.gc.ca/eic/site/012.nsf/eng/h_00008.html

Provincial

Subnational legislation which regulates advocacy and lobbying in Canada can vary from province and territory, but, in comparison to US subnational laws, tends to be more harmonized. Always consult the official and current regulations in your jurisdiction of relevance.

Alberta
No Fee
www.albertalobbyistregistry.ca/

Lobbyist Registrar and General Counsel
(780) 644-3879
Office of the Ethics Commissioner of Alberta
Suite 1250, 9925 - 109 Street NW
Edmonton, Alberta, Canada T5K 2J8
Main Office: (780) 422-2273

British Columbia
No Fee
www.lobbyistsregistrar.bc.ca

Office of the Registrar of Lobbyists for British Columbia
PO Box 9038, Stn. Prov. Govt.
Victoria BC V8W 9A4
Or 4th Floor, 947 Fort Street, Victoria BC V8V 3K3
(250) 387-2686

Manitoba
No Fee
http://lobbyistregistrar.mb.ca

Office of the Lobbyist Registrar for Manitoba
303 - 386 Broadway
Winnipeg, MB, R3C 3R6
(204) 948-3466

New Brunswick
No Fee
https://oic-bci.ca/

Office of the Integrity Commissioner
King's Place
440 King Street, Suite 421
Fredericton, N.B.   E3B 5H8
(506)-457-7890

Newfoundland and Labrador
No Fee
www.gov.nl.ca/dgsnl/registries/lobbyists/

Registry of Lobbyists
Digital Government and Service NL
Commercial Registrations Division
P.O. Box 8700
St. John's, NL A1B 4J6
(709) 729-4043

Commissioner of Lobbyists
120 Conception Bay Highway
Suite 114, Villa Nova Plaza
Conception Bay South, NL A1W 3A6
(709) 834-6159

Nova Scotia

No Fee
http://novascotia.ca/sns/lobbyist/

Registry of Lobbyists
Service Nova Scotia
P.O. Box 1523
Halifax NS B3J 2Y3
(902) 424-5200

Ontario

No Fee
https://www.oico.on.ca/home/lobbyists-registration

Office of the Integrity Commissioner
2 Bloor Street West, Suite 2100
Toronto, ON M4W 3E2
(416)-314-8983

Prince Edward Island

No Fee
www.princeedwardisland.ca/en/information/j
ustice-and-public-safety/prince-edward-island-
lobbyists-registry-overview

Lobbyists Registry
Department of Justice and Public Safety
Consumer, Corporate and Financial Services Division
4th Floor Shaw Building South
95 Rochford Street
PO Box 2000
Charlottetown, PE C1A 7N8
(902) 368-4550

Quebec

No Fee
www.commissairelobby.qc.ca/en

Commissaire au lobbyisme du Québec
900, René-Lévesque Est, bureau 640
Québec, QC G1R 2B5
1-866-281-4615

Saskatchewan

No Fee
www.sasklobbyistregistry.ca/

Office of the Registrar of Lobbyists
Suite 630 – 1855 Victoria Avenue
Regina, SK S4P 3T2
(306)787-0800

Territorial

Nunavut and Northwest Territories currently do not have legislation
that governs advocacy and lobbying.

Yukon

No Fee
https://yukonlobbyistregistry.ca/en

Yukon Legislative Assembly
Box 2703, A-9
Whitehorse, Yukon
Y1A 2C6
(867) 667-5618

LOBBYING LEGISLATION RULES IN THE UNITED STATES

Lobbying has been interpreted by court rulings in the US as constitutionally protected free speech and a way to petition the government for the redress of grievances, two of the freedoms protected by the First Amendment of the Constitution.

Federal

In every legislature in the United States, professional lobbyists must register before lobbying. The federal Lobbying Disclosure Act of 1995 (which replaced the Federal Regulation of Lobbying Act of 1946) established that federal lobbyists be required to register with the Clerk of the US House of Representatives and the Secretary of the US Senate. Anyone failing to do so is punishable by a civil fine of up to $50,000. The clerk and secretary must refer any acts of non-compliance to the United States Attorney for the District of Columbia.

The legislation defines a client as "any person or entity that employs or retains another person for financial or other compensation to conduct lobbying activities on behalf of that person or entity. A person or entity whose employees act as lobbyists on its own behalf is both a client and an employer of such employees."

The term "lobbyist" means "any individual who is employed or retained by a client for financial or other compensation for services that include more than one lobbying contact, other than an individual whose lobbying activities constitute less than 20 percent of the time engaged in the services provided by such individual to that client over a three-month period".

The legislation does not include those lobbyists whose "activities constitute less than 20 percent of the time engaged in services", thus failing to regulate grassroots (small donors) lobbying. The Act includes a number of other "thresholds" that define what must be recorded. Any organization that spends more than $10,000 towards lobbying activities must also be registered. Amounts even slightly below this threshold are exempt from reporting. The outline for registration includes "name, address, business telephone number, and principal place of business of the registrant, and a general description of its business or activities", as well as for the client. The register must also include a statement of what issues the registrant expects to lobby or what may have already been lobbied.

State

Throughout the US, most often lobbyists must file registration paperwork. However, some states require those who hire lobbyists, sometimes called "principals," to file either in addition to lobbyists or instead of them. The definitions of "lobbying" and "lobbyist" also may vary from state to state.

Registration fees range from no fee to several hundred dollars. Some states may require individual lobbyists or lobbying firms to pay filing fees for each client whose interests they represent before the legislature. Registration fees may be waived or reduced for government lobbyists.

The information that needs to be disclosed varies substantially by state. Required information may include the filer's contact and address, client information, and subject matters of interest to the lobbyist's work. A few states may also require photos for ID cards, subcontracted lobbyists, honesty and completeness pledges, or terms of compensation for lobbying work.

A few states may lack substantial detail in the statutes that describe what must be disclosed in lobbyist registration forms. This may mean that the appropriate ethics commission has a substantial degree of discretion in the content, form, and cost of filing.

Source: US government and National Conference of State Legislatures (www.ncsl.org)

GOVERNMENT LINKS FOR LOBBYING IN THE UNITED STATES

Federal

House of Representatives
https://lobbyingdisclosure.house.gov/

Legislative Resource Center
B-81 Cannon House Office Building
Washington, DC 20515
(202) 226-5200

Senate
https://lda.senate.gov/system/public/

Senate Office of Public Records
232 Hart Senate Office Building
Washington, DC 20510
(202) 224-0758

State and Territorial

A comprehensive breakdown of jurisdictions and legislative obligations may be found through:

National Conference of State Legislatures
https://www.ncsl.org/research/ethics/50-
state-chart-lobbyist-registration-
requirements.aspx

NCSL

444 North Capitol Street, N.W., Suite 515
Washington, D.C. 20001
(202)-624-5400

The next section provides a detailed breakdown of the legislative differences among US states and territories as regards the treatment of advocacy and lobbying. The variances among US subnational jurisdictions are considerably more pronounced that those found in Canada, and, accordingly, are detailed to highlight the extent of such differences. Always consult the official and current regulations in your jurisdiction of relevance.

STATE AND TERRITORIAL LOBBYIST REGISTRATION REQUIREMENTS

Alabama
$100
https://alison.legislature.state.al.us/

Registration shall be in writing and contain:
(1) The registrant's full name and business address.
(2) The registrant's normal business and address.
(3) The full name and address of the registrant's principal or principals.
(4) The listing of the categories of subject matters on which the registrant is to communicate directly with a member of the legislative body to influence legislation or legislative action.
(5) If a registrant's activity is done on behalf of the members of a group other than a corporation, a categorical disclosure of the number of persons of the group as: 1-5; 6-10; 11-25; over 25.
(6) A statement signed by each principal that he or she has read the registration, knows its contents and has authorized the registrant to be a lobbyist in his or her behalf as specified therein, and that no compensation will be paid to the registrant contingent upon passage or defeat of any legislative measure.

A registrant shall file a supplemental registration indicating any substantial change or changes in the information contained in the prior registration within 10 days after the date of the change.

Alaska

$250

http://w3.legis.state.ak.us/

The registration form prescribed by the commission must include:

(1) the lobbyist's full name, complete permanent and temporary residence, business address and telephone number;

(2) the full name and complete address of each person by whom the lobbyist is retained or employed;

(3) whether the lobbyist's employer employs the lobbyist solely as a lobbyist or a regular employee performing other services;

(4) the nature or form of the lobbyist's compensation, including salary, fees, or reimbursement for expenses;

(5) a general description of the subjects or matters on which the registrant expects to lobby;

(6) the full name and complete address of the person, if other than the registrant, who has custody of the accounts, books, papers, bills, receipts, and other documents required to be maintained under this chapter;

(7) the identification of a legislative employee or public official to whom the lobbyist is married or who is the domestic partner;

(8) a sworn affirmation by the lobbyist that the lobbyist has completed the training course administered by the commission within the 12-month period preceding the date of registration or registration renewal, excluding a person who is a representational lobbyist;

(9) a sworn affirmation that the lobbyist has not been previously convicted of a felony involving moral turpitude.

Arizona
No more than $25.
https://www.azleg.gov/

Registration, by a principal on behalf of which lobbying may occur, shall contain:
1. The name and business address of the principal.
2. The name and business address of a person who is the designated lobbyist for the principal, regardless of whether such person is engaged to lobby for compensation.
3. The name and business address of each lobbyist for compensation or authorized lobbyist employed by, retained by or representing the principal.
4. For each lobbyist for compensation, designated lobbyist or authorized lobbyist that is not an individual, the name and business address of all employees of that lobbyist who lobby on the principal's behalf.
5. The nature of the primary business or activity, issue, interest or purpose of the principal.
6. The duration of the engagement of any lobbyist.
7. A description of the expenses for which each lobbyist is to be reimbursed by the principal.
8. A listing of the state entities the lobbyist has been engaged or designated to lobby including the legislature and state agencies, boards, commissions or councils.

Registration, by a public body on behalf of which lobbying may occur, shall contain:
1. The name and business address of the public body.
2. The name and business address of a person who is the designated public lobbyist for the public body, regardless of whether this person is engaged to lobby for compensation.

3. The name and business address of each authorized public lobbyist employed by, retained by or representing the public body.
4. For each designated public lobbyist or authorized public lobbyist that is not an individual, the name and business address of all employees of such designated public lobbyist or authorized public lobbyist who may lobby on the public body's behalf.
5. A description of the expenses for which each designated public lobbyist and authorized public lobbyist is to be reimbursed by the public body.

The lobbyist registration form shall include:
1. The name of the lobbyist for compensation, designated lobbyist or designated public lobbyist.
2. The business name and address of the lobbyist for compensation, designated lobbyist or designated public lobbyist.
3. A statement that the lobbyist for compensation, designated lobbyist or designated public lobbyist has read the lobbyist handbook.

Arkansas
No fee specified by statute.
https://www.arkleg.state.ar.us/

Lobbyist registration forms shall contain the following information:
(1) The name, address, and telephone number of the lobbyist;
(2) The calendar year for which the lobbyist is registering;
(3) The types of public servants being lobbied;
(4) The name, address, and telephone number of the lobbyist's client or employer;
(5) A description of the nature of the lobbyist's client or employer; and

(6) Certification by the lobbyist that the information contained on the lobbyist registration form is true and correct.

California
$50
https://leginfo.legislature.ca.gov/

CALIFORNIA REPUBLIC

Lobbyist certification shall include:
  (a) A recent photograph of the lobbyist, in a size prescribed by the Secretary of State.
  (b) Lobbyist's full name, business address, and telephone number.
  (c) A statement that the lobbyist has read and understands the prohibitions contained in Sections 86203 and 86205.
  (d) A statement regarding the lobbyist's completion of the ethics course.
  (e) Any other information the commission requires consistent with this chapter.

Lobbying firm registration shall include:
  (a) The full name, business address, email address and telephone number of the lobbying firm.
  (b) A list of the lobbyists who are partners, owners, officers, or employees of the lobbying firm.
  (c) The lobbyist certification of each lobbyist in the lobbying firm.
  (d) The following info regarding each person with whom the firm has contracts to provide lobbying services: full name, business address, email address, and telephone number, an authorization signed by the person, the time period of the contract, and information sufficient to identify the nature and interests of the person, the lobbying interests of the person, and a list of the state agencies whose legislative or administrative actions the lobbying firm will attempt to influence for the person.
  (e) The name and title of a partner, owner, or officer of the lobbying firm who is responsible for filing statements and reports and

keeping records required by this chapter on behalf of the lobbying firm, and a statement signed by the designated responsible person that he or she has read and understands the prohibitions contained in Sections 86203 and 86205.

(f) Any other information required by the commission consistent with the purposes and provisions of this chapter.

Lobbyist employer registration shall include:

(a) The full name, business address, email address, and telephone number of the lobbyist employer.

(b) A list of the lobbyists who are employed by the lobbyist employer.

(c) The lobbyist certification of each lobbyist employed by the lobbyist employer.

(d) Information sufficient to identify the nature and interests of the filer, including: If the filer is an individual, the name and address of the filer's employer, if any, or his or her principal place of business if the filer is self-employed, and a description of the business activity in which the filer or his or her employer is engaged. If the filer is a business entity, a description of the business activity in which it is engaged. If the filer is an industry, trade, or professional association, a description of the industry, trade, or profession which it represents including a specific description of any portion or faction of the industry, trade, or profession which the association exclusively or primarily represents and, if the association has 50 or fewer members, the names of the members. If the filer is not an individual, business entity, or industry, trade, or professional association, a statement of the person's nature and purposes, including a description of any industry, trade, profession, or other group with a common economic interest which the person principally represents or from which its membership or financial support is principally derived.

(e) The lobbying interests of the lobbyist employer, and a list of the state agencies whose legislative or administrative actions the lobbyist employer will attempt to influence.

(f) Any other information required by the commission consistent with the purposes and provisions of this chapter.

Colorado

Fee amount not specified by statute. Volunteer and not-for-profit lobbyists may be exempt from the fee.

http://leg.colorado.gov/

Professional lobbyists registration shall include:

(a) His or her full legal name, business address, and business telephone number;

(b) The name, address, and telephone number of his or her employer, if applicable;

(c) The name, address, and telephone number of the client for whom he or she will be lobbying; and

(d) The name, address, and telephone number of any other professional lobbyist for whom he or she is lobbying on a subcontract basis.

State Official or State Employee lobbyist registration shall include:

(I) The designated person's full legal name, principal department address, and business telephone number;

(II) The name of any state official or employee who is lobbying on behalf of the principal department, the name of such person's division or unit within the principal department, his classification or job title, and the address and telephone number of his division or unit.

Connecticut

Fee: reasonable fee not in excess of the cost of administering the registration form, not less than $25.

https://www.cga.ct.gov/

If the registrant is an individual, registration must include: the registrant's name, permanent address and temporary address while lobbying and the name, address and nature of business of any person who compensates or reimburses, or agrees to compensate or reimburse the registrant and the terms of the compensation, reimbursement or agreement, but shall not include the compensation paid to an employee for his involvement in activities other than lobbying.

If the registrant is a corporation, the name, address, place of incorporation and the principal place of business of the corporation.
If the registrant is an association, group of persons or an organization, the name and address of the principal officers and directors of such association, group of persons or organization. If the registrant is formed primarily for the purpose of lobbying, it shall disclose the name and address of any person contributing three thousand dollars or more to the registrant's lobbying activities in any calendar year.

If the registrant is not an individual, the name and address of each individual who will lobby on the registrant's behalf.

Registration must also include identification, with reasonable particularity, of areas of legislative or administrative action on which the registrant expects to lobby, including the names of executive agencies and quasi-public agencies and, where applicable, solicitations for state contracts and procurements.

Delaware
Fee amount not specified by statute.
https://legis.delaware.gov/

Lobbyists must register electronically with the following information:
  (1) The name, residence or business address and occupation of each lobbyist;
  (2) The name and business address of the employer of such lobbyist;
  (3) The date on which the employment as lobbyist commenced;
  (4) The length of time the employment is to continue; and
  (5) The subject matter of legislation, regulation or administrative action as to which the employment relates at that time.

District of Columbia
$250. Lobbyists for non-profit organizations pay only $50.
https://dccouncil.us/legislation/

Registration shall include the following information:
  (A) The registrant's name, permanent address, and temporary address while lobbying;
  (B) The name and address of each person who will lobby on the registrant's behalf;
  (C) The name, address, and nature of the business of any person who compensates the registrant and the terms of the compensation; and
  (D) The identification, by formal designation, if known, of matters on which the registrant expects to lobby.

Florida
Fee set annually by a joint rule established by both houses.
http://www.leg.state.fl.us

Lobbying firm filing must include:
Full name, business address, and telephone number of the lobbying firm; Name of each of the firm's lobbyists; and Total compensation provided or owed to the lobbying firm from all principals for the reporting period, reported in one of the following categories: $0; $1 to $49,999; $50,000 to $99,999; $100,000 to $249,999; $250,000 to $499,999; $500,000 to $999,999; $1 million or more. Full name, business address, and telephone number of each principal; and Total compensation provided or owed to the lobbying firm for the reporting period, reported in one of the following categories: $0; $1 to $9,999; $10,000 to $19,999; $20,000 to $29,999; $30,000 to $39,999; $40,000 to $49,999; or $50,000 or more. If the category "$50,000 or more" is selected, the specific dollar amount of compensation must be reported, rounded up or down to the nearest $1,000.

Georgia
No annual fee, but commission shall set, collect and retain fees for lobbyist identification cards, replacements, and supplemental registration.
https://www.legis.ga.gov/

Registration must include the following information:
(1) The applicant's name, address, and telephone number;
(2) The name, address, and telephone number of the person or agency that employs, appoints, or authorizes the applicant to lobby on its behalf;
(3) A statement of the general business or purpose of each person, firm, corporation, association, or agency the applicant represents;

(4) If the applicant represents a membership group other than an agency or corporation, the general purpose and approximate number of members of the organization;

(5) A statement signed by the person or agency employing, appointing, or authorizing the applicant to lobby on its behalf;

(6) If the applicant is a lobbyist attempting to influence rule making or purchasing by a state agency or agencies, the name of the state agency or agencies before which the applicant engages in lobbying;

(7) A statement disclosing each individual or entity on whose behalf the applicant is registering if such individual or entity has agreed to pay him or her an amount exceeding $10,000.00 in a calendar year for lobbying activities;

(8) A statement verifying that the applicant has not been convicted of a felony involving moral turpitude in the courts of this state or an offense that, had it occurred in this state, would constitute a felony involving moral turpitude under the laws of this state or, if the applicant has been so convicted, a statement identifying such conviction, the date thereof, a copy of the person's sentence, and a statement that more than ten years have elapsed since the completion of his or her sentence; and

(9) A statement by the applicant verifying that the applicant has received the Georgia General Assembly Employee Sexual Harassment Policy as set forth in the Georgia General Assembly Handbook, has read and understands the policy, and agrees to abide by the policy.

Guam
Fees not specified by statute.
https://guamlegislature.com/index/

Any person engaged as a lobbyist, before lobbying, shall register with the Legislative Secretary by providing the following information:

(1) name;

(2) business address;

(3) name and address of person by whom they are employed;

(4) interest in which the person appears;

(5) duration of employment;

(6) amount of pay or in-kind compensation including expenses and

(7) names of any papers, periodicals, magazines or other publications wherein lobbyist caused to be published articles or editorials in favor or opposition of pending legislation.

Hawaii
No fee specified by statute.
http://www.capitol.hawaii.gov/

Lobbyists must certify the following information:

(1) The name, mailing address, and business telephone number of the lobbyist.

(2) The name and principal place of business of each person by whom the lobbyist is retained or employed or on whose behalf the lobbyist appears or works and a written authorization to act as a lobbyist from each person by whom the lobbyist is employed or with whom the lobbyist contracts.

(3) The subject areas on which the lobbyist expects to lobby.

Idaho
$10
https://legislature.idaho.gov/

Lobbyist registration shall include:

(1) His name, permanent business address, and any temporary residential and business address in Ada County during the legislative session;

(2) The name, address and general nature of the occupation or business of the lobbyist's employer, and the duration of his employment;

(3) Whether the person from whom he receives compensation employs him solely as a lobbyist or whether he is a regular employee performing services for his employer which include but are not limited to lobbying of legislation;

(4) The general subject or subjects of the lobbyist's legislative interest;

(5) The name and address of the person who will have custody of the accounts, bills, receipts, books, papers, and documents required to be kept under this act.

Illinois
$300
https://www.ilga.gov/

Lobbyist registration must include:

(a) The registrant's name, permanent address, e-mail address, if any, fax number, if any, business telephone number, and temporary address, if the registrant has a temporary address while lobbying. If the registrant is an entity, the information required under subsection (a) for each natural person associated with the registrant who will be lobbying, regardless of whether lobbying is a significant part of his or her duties.

(b) The name and address of the client or clients employing or retaining the registrant to perform such services or on whose behalf the registrant appears. If the client employing or retaining the registrant is a client registrant, the statement shall also include the name and address of the client or clients of the client registrant on whose behalf the registrant will be or anticipates performing services.

(c) A brief description of the executive, legislative, or administrative action in reference to which such service is to be rendered. Each executive and legislative branch agency the registrant expects to lobby during the registration period. The nature of the client's business, by category.

(d) A confirmation that the registrant has a sexual harassment policy, that such policy shall be made available to any individual within two business days upon written request (including electronic requests), that any person may contact the authorized agent of the registrant to report allegations of sexual harassment, and that the registrant recognizes the Inspector General has jurisdiction to review any allegations of sexual harassment alleged against the registrant or lobbyists hired by the registrant.

(e) Each unit of government in the state for which the registrant is or expects to be required to register to lobby the local government during the registration period.

(f) Each elected or appointed office to be held by the registrant at any time during the registration period.

If registrant employees or retains a sub-registrant, statements must include the name and address of the sub-registrant and identify client(s) on behalf the sub-registrant will be performing services.

Indiana
$200, or $100 if a salaried lobbyist for a non-profit organization.
http://iga.in.gov/

The registration statement of each lobbyist who is compensated for lobbying must include the following:

(1) The name, Social Security number, residence address and telephone number, and business address and telephone number of the lobbyist.

(2) The name, business address, telephone number, and kind of business of each person (including the names of each officer or partner) who compensates the lobbyist.

(3) The lobbyist's primary occupation and the name or names of the lobbyist's employers if different than those specified in subdivision.

(4) The subject matter of the lobbyist's lobbying.

(5) The name of any member who is a relative of the lobbyist.

The registration statement of each lobbyist who compensates a person for lobbying must include the following:

(1) The lobbyist's full name, business address and telephone number, kind of business, and the full name of the individual who controls the business, the partners, if any, and officers.

(2) The full name, and business address and telephone number of each person compensated by the lobbyist as a lobbyist.

(3) The subject matter for which the lobbyist has employed or contracted with a lobbyist.

(4) The name of any member who is a relative of the lobbyist.

Iowa

Fees not specified by statute.
https://www.legis.iowa.gov/

Registration must include a statement of all clients of the lobbyist and whether the lobbyist will also be lobbying the executive branch, as well as any other information required by the general assembly.

Kansas

$50/employer if spending $1000 or less and not an employee of a lobbying firm, $350/ employer if spending over $1000 and not an employee of a lobbying firm, $450/lobbyist who is an employee of a lobbying firm.
http://www.kslegislature.org/li/

Registration shall show the name and address of the lobbyist, the name and address of the person compensating the lobbyist for lobbying, the purpose of the employment, the name of each state agency or state office and any agency, division or unit thereof and each judicial department, institution, office, commission, board or bureau and any agency, division or unit thereof and whether the lobbyist will lobby the legislative branch and the method of determining and computing the compensation of the lobbyist. If the lobbyist is compensated or to be compensated for lobbying by more than one employer or is to be engaged in more than one employment, the relevant facts listed above shall be stated separately for each employer and each employment.

Kentucky
$250
https://legislature.ky.gov/

Each legislative agent and employer must file a registration statement listing the following:
  (a) The name, business address and telephone number, and occupation of the legislative agent;
  (b) The name, brief description of the nature of the business, nature and identity of the organized association, coalition, or public interest entity, business address and telephone number of the employer, and the real party in interest on whose behalf the legislative agent is lobbying, if it is different from the employer. For the purposes of this section, if a trade association or other charitable or fraternal organization that is exempt from federal income taxation under Section 501(c) of the Internal Revenue Code is the employer, the statement shall not list the names and addresses of each member of the association or organization, if the association or organization itself is listed;
  (c) The name, bill number, or a brief description of the legislative action for which the legislative agent is or will be engaged in lobbying on behalf of their employer or as a representative of the organized association, coalition, or public interest entity;
  (d) The date on which the legislative agent was engaged; and
  (e) Certification by the employer and legislative agent that the information contained in the registration statement is complete and accurate.

Louisiana
$100
https://legis.la.gov/

Lobbyist registration must include:

(1) Name and business address.

(2) The name and address of each person by whom he is employed and, if different, whose interests he represents, including the business in which that person is engaged.

(3) (a) The name of each person by whom he is paid or is to be paid, the amount he is paid or is to be paid for the purpose of lobbying, and a characterization of such payment as paid, earned but not received, or prospective. (b) Amounts required to be disclosed pursuant to this Paragraph shall be reported by category of value.

(4) (a) An indication of potential subject matters about which he anticipates lobbying. (b) Indication of potential subject matters shall be made by choosing from a list of potential subject matter categories. (c) The unintentional omission of a potential subject matter as provided in this Paragraph shall not be a violation of this Part.

(5) The identity of each legislator or spouse of a legislator with whom he or his employer has, or has had in the preceding twelve months, a business relationship. For purposes of this Paragraph, "business relationship" means any transaction, contract, or activity that is conducted or undertaken for profit and which arises from a joint ownership interest, partnership, or common legal entity between a lobbyist or his employer and a legislator or spouse of a legislator when the legislator or spouse owns ten percent or more of such interest, partnership, or legal entity.

(6) One copy of a two inch by two inch recent photograph of the registrant made within the prior six months shall be filed with the initial registration form for a legislative term.

(7) If a lobbyist is compensated for lobbying and non-lobbying services, he shall reasonably allocate his compensation and report only the amount received for lobbying in the manner provided in this Part.

Maine
$200 for each lobbyist, $100 for each lobbyist associate.
https://legislature.maine.gov/

Lobbyist and employers required to register must include the following information:

1. Names. The name of the lobbyist, a list of the lobbyist associates, the name of the person authorized by the lobbyist to sign the registration and reports for the lobbyist and the name of the person employing the lobbyist;

2. Business addresses. The business address and other contact information for the lobbyist, the lobbyist associates and the person employing the lobbyist;

3. Date. The date upon which lobbying commenced or was expected to commence;

4. Nature of business: A description of the employer's business activity or mission or a description of the industry, trade or profession that the employer represents; Legislative interests: The general areas of legislation that the employer is attempting to influence; Legislative committees: The joint standing committees of the Legislature that the lobbyist expects to lobby during the year; Website of employer: The address for the employer's publicly accessible website; Date of completion of required harassment training: The date that the lobbyist completed the training required under section; and

5. Compensation. The amount of compensation that the lobbyist will receive for that lobbyist's services or, if an exact amount is unascertainable, the basis upon which the lobbyist will charge for those services.

State employee or agency lobbyists required to register must include the following information:

1. Names. The name, business address and contact information of the employee and the department or agency the employee is representing and the address for the publicly accessible website of the department or agency the employee is representing;
2. Position description. A position description;
3. Description of agency. A description of the department or agency the employee is representing, its jurisdiction and its activities; and
4. Legislative interests. The general subject areas of legislation that the department or agency is attempting to influence.

Maryland
$100
https://mgaleg.maryland.gov/

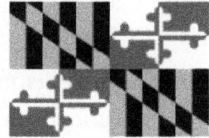

Each registration form, which must be submitted electronically, shall include the following information, if applicable:

(1) the regulated lobbyist's name and permanent address;
(2) the name and permanent address of any other regulated lobbyist that will be lobbying on the regulated lobbyist's behalf;
(3) the name, address, and nature of business of any entity that has engaged the regulated lobbyist for lobbying purposes, accompanied by a statement indicating whether, because of the filing and reporting of the regulated lobbyist, the compensating entity is exempt under § 5-702(c) of this subtitle; and
(4) the identification, by formal designation if known, of the matters on which the regulated lobbyist expects to perform acts, or to engage another regulated lobbyist to perform acts, that require registration under this subtitle.

Massachusetts
$1,000
https://malegislature.gov/

Registration form prescribed by the state secretary. Contents of the registration are not specified by statute.

Michigan
Fee not specified by statute.
https://www.legislature.mi.gov/

Lobbyist registration shall include the following information:
  (a) The name and office address of the lobbyist.
  (b) The name and address of each person employed, reimbursed for expenses which exceed $10.00, or compensated by the lobbyist for lobbying in this state.
  (c) The name, address and nature of business of a person who gives compensation to or reimburses the lobbyist or the representative of a lobbyist for lobbying.
  (d) The fiscal year of the lobbyist.

Lobbyist agent registration shall include the following information:
  (a) The name and office address of the lobbyist agent, if the lobbyist agent is not an individual.
  (b) The name, permanent residence address, and office address of the lobbyist agent, if the lobbyist agent is an individual.
  (c) The name and address of each person employed, reimbursed for expenses, or compensated by the lobbyist agent for lobbying in this state.
  (d) The name, address, and nature of business of a person who gives compensation to or reimburses the lobbyist agent or the representative of a lobbyist agent for lobbying.

HOWEVER: The statute's requirement that registrants disclose identities of persons who contributed to their lobbying organizations unconstitutionally infringed upon free association rights.

Minnesota
Fees: not specified, but a penalty schedule for late or failing to register is provided.
https://www.leg.mn.gov/

Lobbyist registration must include:
(1) the name, address, and e-mail address of the lobbyist;
(2) the principal place of business of the lobbyist;
(3) the name and address of each individual, association, political subdivision, or public higher education system, if any, by whom the lobbyist is retained or employed or on whose behalf the lobbyist appears;
(4) the Web site address of each association, political subdivision, or public higher education system identified under clause (3), if the entity maintains a Web site; and
(5) a general description of the subject or subjects on which the lobbyist expects to lobby. If the lobbyist lobbies on behalf of an association, the registration form must include the name and address of the officers and directors of the association.

Mississippi
Lobbyists and lobbyist clients: $25.
http://www.legislature.ms.gov/

The registration statement shall include the following:
(a) The name, address, occupation and telephone number of the lobbyist;
(b) The name, address, telephone number and principal place of business of the lobbyist's client;
(c) The kind of business of the lobbyist's client;

(d) The full name of the person or persons who control the lobbyist's client, the partners, if any, and officers of the lobbyist's client;

(e) The full name, address and telephone number of each lobbyist employed by or representing the lobbyist's client; and

(f) A statement or statements by the lobbyist and lobbyist's client indicating the specific nature of the issues being advocated for or against on behalf of the lobbyist's client, with sufficient detail so that the precise nature of the lobbyist's advocacy is evident from the statement itself.

Missouri
$10
https://www.mo.gov/

Registration forms shall include the lobbyist's name and business address, the name and address of all persons such lobbyist employs for lobbying purposes, the name and address of each lobbyist principal by whom such lobbyist is employed or in whose interest such lobbyist appears or works.

Montana
$150, subject to a hardship, waived if annual lobbying compensation is less than $2,150.
https://leg.mt.gov/

Registration information required to be supplied is not specified by statute, but includes the name and business address of each lobbyist, the name and business address of the lobbyist's principal, and the subject or subjects to which the employment relates or a statement that the employment relates to all matters in which the principal has an interest.

Nebraska

$200 for each principal, and $15 for each principal if unpaid.
https://nebraskalegislature.gov/

The registration statement shall include the following:

(1) The name, permanent residence address, and office address of the lobbyist;

(2) The name and address of the principal of such lobbyist;

(3) The nature of the business of such principal and the amounts or sums given or to be given the lobbyist as compensation or reimbursement for lobbying. A lobbyist who is salaried or retained by a principal need only report that portion of compensation or reimbursement reasonably attributable to lobbying;

(4) A description of the business activity of the lobbyist;

(5) An identification of the matters on which the principal or lobbyist expects to lobby;

(6) If the principal is an industry, trade, or professional association, a specific description of the industry, trade, or profession represented by the principal and the names and addresses of its officers;

(7) If the principal is not an industry, trade, or professional association, a specific description of the interests and groups represented by the principal and the names and addresses of its officers; and

(8) The name and address of any official in the legislative or executive branch, and of any members of any such official's staff or immediate family, who are employed by the lobbyist or any person acting on behalf of such lobbyist if such information is known or reasonably should have been known to the lobbyist.

Nevada

Fee not specified by statute, but authorizes the
Legislative Commission to establish fees.
https://www.leg.state.nv.us/

The registration statement of a lobbyist must contain the following information:

1. The registrant's full name, permanent address, place of business and temporary address while lobbying.

2. The full name and complete address of each person, if any, by whom the registrant is retained or employed or on whose behalf the registrant appears.

3. A listing of any direct business associations or partnerships involving any current Legislator and the registrant or any person by whom the registrant is retained or employed. The listing must include any such association or partnership constituting a source of income or involving a debt or interest in real estate required to be disclosed in a financial disclosure statement made by a public officer or candidate.

4. The name of any current Legislator for whom the registrant, or any person by whom the registrant is retained or employed, has, in connection with a political campaign of the Legislator, provided consulting, advertising or other professional services since the beginning of the preceding regular session.

5. A description of the principal areas of interest on which the registrant expects to lobby.

6. If the registrant lobbies or purports to lobby on behalf of members, a statement of the number of members.

7. A declaration under penalty of perjury that none of the registrant's compensation or reimbursement is contingent, in whole or in part, upon the production of any legislative action.

New Hampshire
$50 for each person lobbying for each reported client or employer.
http://www.gencourt.state.nh.us/

The lobbyist registration shall be on a form prescribed by the secretary of state that shall at a minimum include:

(a) The full name of the person registering, if that person is affiliated with a partnership, firm, or corporation, the name of that partnership, firm, or corporation, the name of the client who has employed the person registering, his or her respective business addresses, or if none, his or her residence address.

(b) The usual occupation or primary field of business of each.

(c) The date and character of the employment or agreement therefor.

(d) The duration of the employment if it can be determined.

(e) The special subjects of legislation or executive branch action, if any, to which the employment relates.

(f) If the person registering is a member of or affiliated with a partnership, firm, or corporation that has other members or employees who are also registered as a lobbyist, a list of the full name of each such person. Being listed in this subparagraph does not relieve anyone who will be lobbying for this client from being listed individually under subparagraph (a).

(g) The following statement followed by a line for each person filing the form to sign and date the form: "I have read RSA 15 and hereby swear or affirm that the foregoing information is true and complete to the best of my knowledge and belief."

New Jersey
Fees set by the ethics commission.
https://www.njleg.state.nj.us/

Registration filing must include the following information:

(1) his name, business address and regular occupation;

(2) name, business address and occupation or principal business of the person from whom he receives compensation for acting as a governmental affairs agent;

(3) (a) name, business address and occupation or principal business of any person in whose interest he acts as a governmental affairs agent in consideration of the aforesaid compensation, if such person is other than the person from whom said compensation is received; and

(b) if a person, identified under paragraph (2) of this subsection as one from whom the governmental affairs agent receives compensation, is a membership organization or corporation whose name or occupation so identified does not, either explicitly or by virtue of the nature of the principal business in which the organization or its members, or the corporation or its shareholders, is commonly known to be engaged, clearly reveal the primary specific economic, social, political, or other interest which the organization or corporation may reasonably be understood to seek to advance or protect through its employment, retainer, or engagement of the governmental affairs agent, a description of that primary economic, social, political, or other interest and a list of the persons having organizational or financial control of the organization or corporation, including the names, mailing addresses and occupations, respectively, of those persons. The commission shall promulgate rules and regulations to govern the content of any information required to be disclosed under this subparagraph and shall take such steps as are reasonably necessary to ensure that all such information is, in accordance with those rules and regulations, both accurate and complete. Any list of governmental affairs agents and their principals required to be published quarterly shall include, for each such principal for whom it is not otherwise apparent, the primary specific interest which the principal may reasonably be understood to seek to advance or protect through its engagement of the governmental affairs agent and the category of persons required to file additional information, as that interest and such category shall have been determined under subparagraph (b) of this paragraph;

(4) whether the person from whom he receives said compensation employs him solely as a governmental affairs agent, or whether he is a regular employee performing services for his employer which include but are not limited to the influencing of legislation, regulation or governmental processes;

(5) the length of time for which he will be receiving compensation from the person aforesaid for acting as a governmental affairs agent, if said length of time can be ascertained at the time of filing;

(6) the type of legislation, regulation or governmental process or the particular legislation, regulation or governmental process in relation to which he is to act as governmental affairs agent in consideration of the aforesaid compensation, and any particular legislation, regulation or governmental process or type of legislation, regulation or governmental process which he is to promote or oppose;

(8) When a governmental affairs agent is employed or retained by any State or local government agency, department, board, bureau, commission, authority, board of education, institution of higher education, or any other government entity in this State, the notice of representation shall also indicate the compensation amount received or to be received by the governmental affairs agent from the government entity. Each notice of representation indicating that the governmental affairs agent is employed or retained by a government entity shall be posted by the commission on the commission's Internet site within 30 days of filing, and shall be easily available for public inspection through that Internet site.

New Mexico
$50
https://www.nmlegis.gov/

Registration shall include: (1) the lobbyist's full name, permanent business address and business address while lobbying; and (2) the name and address of each of the lobbyist's employers.

New York
$50
https://nyassembly.gov/

Statement of registration shall contain:
   (1) name, address and telephone number of the lobbyist, and if the lobbyist is an organization the names, addresses and telephone numbers of any officer or employee of such lobbyist who engages in any lobbying activities or who is employed in an organization's division that engages in lobbying activities of the organization;
   (2) name, address and telephone number of the client by whom or on whose behalf the lobbyist is retained, employed or designated;
   (3) if such lobbyist is retained or employed pursuant to a written agreement of retainer or employment, a copy of such shall also be attached and if such retainer or employment is oral, a statement of the substance thereof; such written retainer, or if it is oral, a statement of the substance thereof, and any amendment thereto, shall be retained for 3 years;
   (4) a written authorization from the client by whom the lobbyist is authorized to lobby, unless such lobbyist has filed a written agreement of retainer or employment pursuant to paragraph three of this subdivision;
   (5) the following information on which the lobbyist expects to lobby: (i) a description of the general subject or subjects, (ii) the

legislative bill numbers of any bills, (iii) the numbers or subject matter (if there are no numbers) of gubernatorial executive orders or executive orders issued by the chief executive officer of a municipality, (iv) the subject matter of and tribes involved in tribal-state compacts, memoranda of understanding, or any other state-tribal agreements and any state actions related to class III gaming as provided in 25 U.S.C. § 2701, (v) the rule, regulation, and ratemaking numbers of any rules, regulations, rates, or municipal ordinances and resolutions, or proposed rules, regulations, or rates, or municipal ordinances and resolutions, and (vi) the titles and any identifying numbers of any procurement contracts and other documents disseminated by a state agency, either house of the state legislature, the unified court system, municipal agency or local legislative body in connection with a governmental procurement;

(6) name of the person, organization, or legislative body before which the lobbyist is lobbying or expects to lobby;

(7) if the lobbyist is retained, employed or designated by more than one client, a separate statement of registration shall be required for each such client.

(8) (i) the name and public office address of any statewide elected official, state officer or employee, member of the legislature or legislative employee and entity with whom the lobbyist has a reportable business relationship; (ii) a description of the general subject or subjects of the transactions between the lobbyist or lobbyists and the statewide elected official, state officer or employee, member of the legislature or legislative employee and entity; and (iii) the compensation, including expenses, to be paid and paid by virtue of the business relationship.

North Carolina

Lobbyists, with a separate registration for each principal: $250.
www.ncleg.gov

The form of the registration shall be prescribed by the Secretary of State, be filed electronically, and shall include the registrant's full name, firm, complete address, and telephone number; the registrant's place of business; the full name, complete address, and telephone number of each principal the lobbyist represents; and a general description of the matters on which the registrant expects to act as a lobbyist.

North Dakota
$25 per lobbyist and the first principal, $15 for each subsequent principal after the first.
https://www.ndlegis.gov/

The registrant shall state in writing:
(1) The registrant's full name and business address; and
(2) The name and address of any person upon whose behalf the registrant appears, any person in whose interest the registrant appears or works, the duration of the employment or appearances, and by whom the registrant is paid or is to be paid.

Ohio
$25
https://www.legislature.ohio.gov/

Registration must include:
(1) The name, business address, and occupation of the legislative agent;
(2) The name and business address of the employer and the real party in interest on whose behalf the legislative agent is actively advocating, if it is different from the employer. For the purposes of division of this section, where a trade association or other charitable or fraternal organization that is exempt from federal income taxation under subsection 501(c) of the federal Internal Revenue Code is the employer, the statement need not list the names and addresses of each member of the association or

organization, so long as the association or organization itself is listed.

(3) A brief description of the type of legislation to which the engagement relates.

Oklahoma
$100
http://www.oklegislature.gov/

Contents of registration not specified by statute. Contents of registration is deferred to the Ethics Commission.

Oregon
No fee for electronic filing.
https://www.oregonlegislature.gov/

Registration shall contain the following:

(a) The name, address, electronic mail address and telephone number of the lobbyist.

(b) The name, address, electronic mail address and telephone number of each person that employs the lobbyist or in whose interest the lobbyist appears or works.

(c) A general description of the trade, business, profession or area of endeavor of any person designated under paragraph (b) of this subsection, and a statement by the person that the lobbyist is officially authorized to lobby for the person.

(d) The name of any member of the Legislative Assembly employed, retained or otherwise compensated by: (A) The lobbyist designated under paragraph (a) of this subsection; or (B) A person designated under paragraph (b) of this subsection.

(e) The general subject or subjects of the legislative action of interest to the person for whom the lobbyist is registered.

Pennsylvania
$100
https://www.legis.state.pa.us/

A principal or lobbying firm shall provide the following information:

(i) Name.

(ii) Permanent address.

(iii) Daytime telephone number.

(iv) E-mail address, if available.

(v) Name and nature of business.

(vi) Name, registration number and acronym of any affiliated political action committees.

(vii) Name and permanent business address of each individual who will for economic consideration engage in lobbying on behalf of the principal or lobbying firm.

(viii) Registration number when available.

A lobbying firm shall include in its statement the following information for each principal it represents:

(i) Name.

(ii) Permanent business address.

(iii) Telephone number.

(iv) Registration number when available. A principal that is an association or organization shall include in its statement the number of dues-paying members of the association or organization in the most recently completed calendar year.

A lobbyist who is required to register shall file a single registration statement setting forth the following information with the department:

(1) Name.

(2) Permanent business address.

(3) Daytime telephone number.

(4) E-mail address, if available.

(5) A recent photograph of the lobbyist.

(6) Name, permanent business address, daytime telephone number and registration number when available of each principal for whom the lobbyist will engage in lobbying.

(7) Name and registration number when available of any lobbying firm with which the lobbyist has a relationship involving economic consideration.

(8) Name, registration number and acronym of any affiliated political action committees.

(9) Name, registration number and acronym of any candidate political committee of which the lobbyist is an officer who must be included in a registration statement under section 1624(b)(2) and (3) of the act of June 3, 1937 (P.L. 1333, No. 320),1 known as the Pennsylvania Election Code.

Puerto Rico

Statutes specifying registration requirements were not found. Registration requirements may be specified in House and Senate rules.
https://www.oslpr.org/

Statutes specifying registration requirements not found. Registration requirements may be specified in House and Senate rules.

Rhode Island

Lobbyists. Fees not specified by statute.
https://www.rilegislature.gov/

Registration must include:

(1) Name and address of the lobbyist(s);

(2) The legislation by bill number or by the subject matter(s) of the lobbying;

(3) The executive branch officials or public bodies to be lobbied;

(4) Compensation, except for those lobbyists employed by a lobbying firm; and

(5) Any other information required by the secretary. Governmental lobbyists exempted from requirements 2 through 5.

South Carolina
$100
https://www.scstatehouse.gov/

The registration must be in a form prescribed by the State Ethics Commission and be limited to and contain:

(1) the lobbyist's full name and address, telephone number, occupation, name of employer, principal place of business, and position held in that business by the lobbyist;

(2) an identification of the public office or public body which the lobbyist will engage in lobbying and the subject matter in which the lobbyist will engage in lobbying, including the name of legislation, covered agency actions, or covered gubernatorial actions, if known; and

(3) certification by the lobbyist that the information contained on the registration statement is true and correct.

(4) If a lobbyist fails to identify the public office or public body for which he is authorized to engage in lobbying, as required by item (2) of this subsection, then the lobbyist's principal for whom the lobbyist is authorized to engage in lobbying is deemed a lobbyist's principal as to all public offices or public bodies of the State.

South Dakota
Fees set by the secretary of state but not to exceed $65.
https://sdlegislature.gov/

Does not specifically prescribe what information must be disclosed or provided in a registration form, but the law requires that the secretary of state prepare and keep a directory of registered lobbyists that contain the following information, likely to be required at the time of registration: The directory shall contain the name and business address of the employer, the name, residence, and occupation of the person employed, the date of the employment or agreement therefor, the length of time the employment is to continue, if such time can be determined, and the special subject or subjects of legislation, if any, to which the employment relates.

Tennessee
Fees established by rule not set by statute.
https://capitol.tn.gov/

Each employer of a lobbyist shall electronically file a registration statement that includes the following information:
(A) Employer's name, business address, telephone number and e-mail address; and, in the case of a corporation, association or governmental entity, the names of the individuals performing the functions of chief executive officer and chief financial officer;
(B) Name, business address, telephone number and e-mail address of each lobbyist authorized to represent the employer; and
(C) Verification that the employer has downloaded from the commission web site or otherwise obtained the commission's manual for lobbyists and employers of lobbyists.

Each lobbyist shall electronically file a registration statement that includes the following information:
(A) Lobbyist's name, business address, telephone number and e-mail address;
(B) Name, business address, telephone number and e-mail address of each employer the lobbyist is authorized to represent;
(C) Subject matters lobbied for such employers during the registration year, to be indicated among general categories listed by the ethics commission;

(D) Name and business address of any member of the lobbyist's immediate family who is an official within the legislative or executive branch; and

(E) The extent of any direct business arrangement or partnership between the lobbyist and any candidate for public office or any official in the legislative or executive branch.

Texas
$150 for non-profits; $75 for any person who must register only for reimbursement of expenses; $750 for all others.
https://capitol.texas.gov/

The registration must be written and verified and must contain:

(1) the registrant's full name and address;

(2) the registrant's normal business, business phone number, and business address;

(3) the full name and address of each person: (A) who reimburses, retains, or employs the registrant to communicate directly with a member of the legislative or executive branch to influence legislation or administrative action; and (B) on whose behalf the registrant has communicated directly with a member of the legislative or executive branch to influence legislation or administrative action;

(4) the subject matter of the legislation or of the administrative action that is the subject of the registrant's direct communication with a member of the legislative or executive branch and, if applicable, the docket number or other administrative designation of the administrative action;

(5) for each person employed or retained by the registrant for the purpose of assisting in direct communication with a member of the legislative or executive branch to influence legislation or administrative action: (A) the full name, business address, and occupation of the person; and (B) the subject matter of the legislation or of the administrative action to which the person's

activities reportable under this section were related and, if applicable, the docket number or other administrative designation of the administrative action; and

(6) the amount of compensation or reimbursement paid by each person who reimburses, retains, or employs the registrant for the purpose of communicating directly with a member of the legislative or executive branch or on whose behalf the registrant communicates directly with a member of the legislative or executive branch.

Utah
$110
https://le.utah.gov/

The lieutenant governor shall prepare a Lobbyist License Application Form that includes:

(i) a place for the lobbyist's name and business address;

(ii) a place for the following information for each principal for whom the lobbyist works or is hired as an independent contractor: (A) the principal's name; (B) the principal's business address; (C) the name of each public official that the principal employs and the nature of the employment with the public official; and (D) the general purposes, interests, and nature of the principal;

(iii) a place for the name and address of the person who paid or will pay the lobbyist's registration fee, if the fee is not paid by the lobbyist;

(iv) a place for the lobbyist to disclose: (A) any elected or appointed position that the lobbyist holds in state or local government, if any; and (B) the name of each public official that the lobbyist employs and the nature of the employment with the public official, if any;

(v) a place for the lobbyist to disclose the types of expenditures for which the lobbyist will be reimbursed; and

(vi) a certification to be signed by the lobbyist that certifies that the information provided in the form is true, accurate, and complete to the best of the lobbyist's knowledge and belief. Must take harassment training prior to registration as a lobbyist.

Vermont

$60 for lobbyists, $15 for employers.
https://legislature.vermont.gov/

A registration statement filed by a lobbyist shall be signed by the lobbyist and shall contain the following information:
  (1) The name, mailing address, and telephone number of the lobbyist.
  (2) The name of the employer and date of employment for the biennium.
  (3) A description of the matters for which lobbying has been engaged by the employer.
  (4) If a lobbyist is compensated, in whole or in part, by an employer for the purpose of lobbying on behalf of another person or group or coalition, the lobbyist shall provide the name of the employer, the name of the person, group, or coalition on whose behalf he or she lobbies, and a description of the matters for which lobbying has been engaged by the employer.
  (5) A current passport-type photograph of the lobbyist.
  (6) All subject areas for which lobbying is performed.

A registration statement filed by an employer shall be signed by the employer and shall contain the following information:
  (1) the name of the employer;
  (2) the trade name, if any, of the employer;
  (3) the mailing address and the telephone number of the employer;
  (4) the contact person for the employer;
  (5) the name and mailing address of each lobbyist engaged by the employer and date of employment or contract for the biennium.

Virgin Islands
Statutes specifying registration requirements not found.
https://www.legvi.org/

Statutes specifying registration requirements were not found.

Virginia
$100 per principal.
https://virginiageneralassembly.gov/

The registration statement shall be on a form provided by the Secretary of the Commonwealth and include the following information:

1. The name and business address and telephone number of the lobbyist;
2. The name and business address and telephone number of the person who will keep custody of the lobbyist's and the lobbyist's principal's accounts and records required to comply with this article, and the location and telephone number for the place where the accounts and records are kept;
3. The name and business address and telephone number of the lobbyist's principal;
4. The kind of business of the lobbyist's principal;
5. For each principal, the full name of the individual to whom the lobbyist reports;
6. For each principal, a statement whether the lobbyist is employed or retained and whether exclusively for the purpose of lobbying;
7. The position held by the lobbyist if he is a part-time or full-time employee of the principal;
8. An identification of the subject matter (with as much specificity as possible) with regard to which the lobbyist or lobbyist's principal will engage in lobbying; and
9. The statement of the lobbyist, which shall be signed either originally or by electronic signature as authorized by the

Uniform Electronic Transactions Act, that the information contained on the registration statement is true and correct.

Washington
Fee not specified by statute.
https://leg.wa.gov/

Registration must include the following information:

(a) The lobbyist's name, permanent business address, and any temporary residential and business addresses in Thurston county during the legislative session;

(b) The name, address and occupation or business of the lobbyist's employer;

(c) The duration of the lobbyist's employment;

(d) The compensation to be received for lobbying, the amount to be paid for expenses, and what expenses are to be reimbursed;

(e) Whether the lobbyist is employed solely as a lobbyist or whether the lobbyist is a regular employee performing services for his or her employer which include but are not limited to the influencing of legislation;

(f) The general subject or subjects to be lobbied;

(g) A written authorization from each of the lobbyist's employers confirming such employment;

(h) The name and address of the person who will have custody of the accounts, bills, receipts, books, papers, and documents required to be kept under this chapter;

(i) If the lobbyist's employer is an entity (including, but not limited to, business and trade associations) whose members include, or which as a representative entity undertakes lobbying activities for, businesses, groups, associations, or organizations, the name and address of each member of such entity or person represented by such entity whose fees, dues, payments, or other consideration paid to such entity during either of the prior two years have exceeded *five hundred dollars or who is obligated to or has agreed to pay fees, dues, payments, or other consideration exceeding *five hundred dollars to such entity during the current year; and

(j) an attestation that the lobbyist has read and completed a training course regarding the legislative code of conduct and any policies related to appropriate conduct adopted by the senate or house of representatives.

West Virginia
$100, plus $100 per each principal.
http://www.wvlegislature.gov/

Registration information must include:
(1) The registrant's name, business address, telephone numbers and any temporary residential and business addresses and telephone numbers used or to be used by the registrant while lobbying during a legislative session;

(2) The name, address and occupation or business of the registrant's employer;

(3) A statement as to whether the registrant is employed or retained by his or her employer solely as a lobbyist or is a regular employee performing services for the employer which include, but are not limited to, lobbying;

(4) A statement as to whether the registrant is employed or retained by his or her employer under any agreement, arrangement or understanding according to which the registrant's compensation, or any portion of the registrant's compensation, is or will be contingent upon the success of his or her lobbying activity;

(5) The general subject or subjects, if known, on which the registrant will lobby or employ some other person to lobby in a manner which requires registration under this article; and

(6) An appended written authorization from each of the lobbyist's employers confirming the lobbyist's employment and the subjects on which the employer is to be represented.

Wisconsin

Principals spending over $500 per year: Fee: $250/1principal, $400/2 or more principals. Subject to a veterans waiver.

https://legis.wisconsin.gov/

Registration must include the registrant's social security number or driver's license number and an affirmation that the registration is true under penalty of perjury. Wis. Stat. Ann. § 13.63. Principal registration must include the principal's name, business address, the general areas of legislative and administrative action which the principal is attempting to influence, the names of any agencies in which the principal seeks to influence administrative action, and information sufficient to identify the nature and interest of the principal. Must also include:

(a) If the principal is an individual, the name and address of the individual's employer, if any, or the individual's principal place of business if self-employed, a description of the business activity in which the individual or the individual's employer is engaged and, the individual's social security number.

(b) If a business entity, a description of the business activity in which the principal is engaged and the name of its chief executive officer, or in the case of a partnership or limited liability company the names of the partners or members.

(c) If an industry, trade or professional association, a description of the industry, trade or profession which it represents including a specific description of any segment or portion of the industry, trade or profession which the association exclusively or primarily represents and the name of the chief executive officer and the approximate number of its members.

(d) If not an individual, business entity or industry, trade or professional association, a statement of the principal's nature and purposes, including a description of any industry, trade, profession or other group with a common interest which the principal primarily represents or from which its membership or financial support is primarily derived and the approximate number of its members.

(e) The name and position or relationship to the principal of any designee who is authorized to sign other documents.

Wyoming
$25
https://www.wyoleg.gov/

Registration shall state:
(i) The name and business address of the individual registering;
(ii) The name and business address of the association, corporation, labor union, public, non-profit or private special interest group which the person represents.

PLANNING
JOURNAL

Is your lobbying registration accurate and current?

Do you need to register with other governments
or legislatures?

What exactly are you trying to achieve? Do you want to introduce, change, oppose or eliminate something?

Have you ever met with a public office holder, and neither the meeting nor its proceedings were made public? Your advocacy might have fallen into the regulated category of lobbying.

> *Remember: advocacy takes time, sometimes years.*

Reference the name and number of a bill only while it is a bill, when it represents proposed legislation. After it becomes law, the bill number is less relevant, so, as a matter of minimizing confusion, refer to the name and statute number of the act that it has evolved into.

> *Never reiterate or simply read your written submission to a government committee. The committee already has it, so your verbal presentation must complement, not reiterate.*

Special events, receptions and advocacy/lobby days really are mini conferences. Plan and prepare accordingly.

> *Define your message clearly, focusing on do-ability, while avoiding gimmickry.*

Routinely ensure the accuracy of your contact and outreach lists.

Periodically ask yourself two questions: "Are we successful in our advocacy efforts?" and "How do we know?"

Diarize your interactions and communications with all public officials throughout your advocacy work.

> *A legislator will respect you and your issue more if you respect their time and schedule.*

> The staffers in a political or legislative office are just as important as the formally elected representative. Many of those staff members are representatives-in-waiting.

Always try to be helpful. As you ask the elected representative for assistance or support, also ask that person if there is anything you can do to help.

Avoid sector-based lingo and buzzwords.

> *Advocacy is a form of content creation, promotion and persuasion, to move the "needle" from what is to what ought to be.*

Never assume that the public official knows your issue to the extent that you do.

Is your lobbying registration accurate and current?

Do you need to register with other governments or legislatures?

> *What exactly are you trying to achieve? Do you want to introduce, change, oppose or eliminate something?*

Have you ever met with a public office holder,
and neither the meeting nor its proceedings
were made public? Your advocacy might have
fallen into the regulated category of lobbying.

> *Remember: advocacy takes time, sometimes years.*

Reference the name and number of a bill only while it is a bill, when it represents proposed legislation. After it becomes law, the bill number is less relevant, so, as a matter of minimizing confusion, refer to the name and statute number of the act that it has evolved into.

> *Never reiterate or simply read your written submission to a government committee. The committee already has it, so your verbal presentation must complement, not reiterate.*

Special events, receptions and advocacy/lobby days really are mini conferences. Plan and prepare accordingly.

Define your message clearly, focusing on do-ability, while avoiding gimmickry.

Routinely ensure the accuracy of your contact and outreach lists.

> *Periodically ask yourself two questions: "Are we successful in our advocacy efforts?" and "How do we know?"*

A legislator will respect you and your issue more if you respect their time and schedule.

The staffers in a political or legislative office are just as important as the formally elected representative. Many of those staff members are representatives-in-waiting.

Always try to be helpful. As you ask the elected representative for assistance or support, also ask that person if there is anything you can do to help.

Avoid sector-based lingo and buzzwords.

Advocacy is a form of content creation, promotion and persuasion, to move the "needle" from what is to what ought to be.

> *Never assume that the public official knows your issue to the extent that you do.*

Get Your Copy of *Advocacy: Explained!* at an Amazon Global Marketplace today!

www.henleypoint.ca

Henley Point Productions 2022

ABOUT THE AUTHOR

Steven Christianson's career experience spans Canada's Parliament and the United Nations, the corporate and non-profit sectors. For several years he taught advocacy as an instructor with Ryerson University in Toronto. A public policy analyst by vocation, and an avid podcaster and content creator, his work is defined by developing content, promoting it, and making it work.

Steven's professional career has focused on government relations and advocacy, public relations and political management.

Steven holds a Master's degree in public policy and political economy. He is the author of a special edition book, *Canada's Indian Act: Policy Perspectives from the Years Defined by Oka, Meech Lake and the Royal Commission*, as well as the *Explained!* series, titles which include *Content Creation and Promotion*, *Podcasting*, and *Advocacy*.

Steven has one daughter, Courtney, and lives in Toronto with his wife, Josée, and two cats, Sophie and Jules.

9 781777 834708